D1150097

SUGAR
COUNTER

HOW TO SHOP
WITHOUT SUGAR

Some of the nutrient information has been calculated using data from the UK Food Nutrient Databank which is available from The Food Standards Agency (FSA). Other values have either been estimated based on similar foods or obtained from relevant manufacturers. Whilst every effort has been made to ensure that all nutritional information given is accurate at the time of publication, errors may occur. With thanks also to Marks & Spencer, KFC and McDonalds press offices who provided product information direct to the author.

This book is meant to be used as a general reference guide. The information in this book is intended only as a guide to following a healthy diet. People with special dietary requirements of any kind should consult appropriate medical professionals before changing their diet. Whilst all reasonable care has been taken during the preparation of this edition, neither the publisher nor author can accept any responsibility for any consequences arising from the use of this information.

An Hachette UK Company

www.hachette.co.uk

First published in Great Britain in 2014 by Hamlyn,
a division of Octopus Publishing Group Ltd

Endeavour House 189 Shaftesbury Avenue London WC2H 8JY

www.octopusbooks.co.uk

Copyright © Octopus Publishing Group Ltd 2014

All rights reserved. No part of this work may be reproduced or utilized in any form or by any means, electronic or mechanical, including photocopying, recording or by any information storage and retrieval system, without the prior written permission of the publisher.

ISBN 978-0-600-63037-1

A CIP catalogue record for this book is available from the British Library

Printed and bound in Spain

10 9 8 7 6 5 4 3 2 1

Sugar Counter App Now Available on

Available on the App Store

amazon apps Available on kindle fire

ANDROID APP ON Google play

nook by Barnes & Noble

Windows Phone

http://bit.ly/sugarcounter

SUGAR
COUNTER

HOW TO SHOP
WITHOUT SUGAR

OVER 1400 ANALYSED FOODS AND BRANDS

Angela Dowden

hamlyn

CONTENTS

Introduction

Like it or lump it, sugar is a health baddy that we should all be aware of and strive to cut down in our diets. But that can be easier said than done because, as well as the obvious sources like sugary drinks, cakes and biscuits, sugar is present in many less obvious places from supermarket ready meals to soups and sauces. Overall, just 17 per cent of the sugar we consume comes from the packet sugar that we sprinkle or the preserves that we spread; the rest occurs in a vast selection of everyday supermarket foods that make their way into our shopping trolleys every week.

In this book, we've listed over 1400 different branded and generic everyday foods with at-a-glance information on sugar content (per portion, teaspoon equivalents and per 100g), plus subsidiary information on other important dietary components that you may want to keep in check – saturates, salt and calories. Use it as your pocket companion when you shop and you will soon learn the food swaps to make for a healthier diet and to ensure you aren't eating too much of the sweet stuff.

WHY DO WE LIKE SUGAR SO MUCH?

One theory is that a sweeter taste indicated to our ancestors foods that were safer to eat and a good source of energy. Our very first food – breast or formula milk – is also naturally sweet and we can quickly come to associate sweetness with comfort and reward in early childhood. All these factors conspire to give many of us a very sweet tooth!

Why is sugar bad?

One of the main issues with sugar is that it is a very palatable source of calories that slips down all too easily, often without filling you up much. The campaign group Action on Sugar, set up by experts in January 2014, says that a 20–30 per cent reduction in sugar added by the food industry – a goal they are pushing for within 3–5 years – would result in a reduction in energy intake of approximately 100 calories per day. According to their calculations, this reduction in sugar could be predicted to stall the current rise in obesity.

Some evidence suggests that sugar is bad for us independent of its contribution to obesity. For example, a recent *JAMA Internal Medicine* study (published by the American Medical Association) revealed that people who got a quarter of their calories from added sugar (two and a half times more than is recommended) trebled their risk of heart disease compared with people who got 10 per cent of their calories from added sugar. Another research study that looked at sugar consumption in 175 countries, found that for every additional 150 calories of sugar available per person per day, the prevalence of diabetes in the population rose by 1 per cent. In comparison, 150 calories of any type was correlated with only a 0.1 per cent increase in the population's diabetes rate.

The theory goes that because a high-sugar diet requires the pancreas to pump out higher and more frequent amounts of insulin, the body can become resistant to the hormone, and more at risk of diabetes, fatty liver and heart disease. Being overweight, inactive and apple shaped are likely to exacerbate the negative effects of sugar.

Food and drinks that have a lot of added sugars will also often have few other nutrients. And sugary foods and drinks can cause tooth decay, especially if you eat them between meals. The longer the sugary food is in contact with the teeth, the more damage it can cause.

Is it possible to be addicted to sugar?

Research has found that consuming sugar fires up reward areas of the brain, causing the release of feel-good dopamine. However, while it's certainly fashionable to draw parallels between sugar and addictive drugs, the most that can currently be said is that drugs and pleasurable food components such as sugar (but also other enjoyable activities or emotions like listening to beautiful music or being in love) act on common neural pathways. To say that we can have a physical dependency on sugar in the same way as some people might on heroin, is a stretch too far according to most experts.

That said, some people do exhibit addictive-like behaviour around sugary foods and will repeatedly use sugar as a 'fix' for both a physical

KNOW YOUR SPOONS

General guidelines for the measurement of sugar per spoonful are as follows

1 level teaspoon = 4g
1 heaped teaspoon = 6g

preserves and fruit juices, in which the sugar is not incorporated within the cell structure of a food.

These sugars are more likely to do harm, as they are available to the body in higher concentrations and often without the benefit of fibre, which slows absorption into the blood stream.

and a mental lift. The fact that sugar tends to give an immediate boost in blood sugar, followed by a rapid fall can only add to this roller-coaster effect of energy and emotions.

Very problematic sugar cravings are often indicative of deep-rooted issues with food in general, and in the worst case scenario may require some sort of psychological change, such as hypnotherapy or a dietitian-led programme on intuitive eating, as well as a general diet overhaul.

'Added' versus natural

Though we talk about 'sugar' in general there are actually two types – 'added' and natural.

'Added sugars' (sometimes also referred to by nutritionists as 'non-milk extrinsic' sugars) don't just include the sugar we sprinkle or the sugar added during the manufacture of foods, but also honeys, syrups,

How much sugar should we have?

Current UK guidelines suggest added sugars shouldn't make up more than 10 per cent of the energy we get from food. That's around 50g or 12.5 × 4g teaspoons per day as a daily maximum for women (one 500ml bottle of cola will get you to this limit) and 70g a day or 17.5 teaspoons a day for men. For children over ten the limit is around the same as for women; children under this age should have less.

The naturally occurring sugars in milk, vegetables and whole (non-juiced) fruits are deemed to be more innocuous, and current recommendations are that we can eat up to a guideline daily amount (GDA) of 90g a day of sugar in total (120g for men) as long as the added sugar component is kept to the 50g–70g figure mentioned above.

Obviously these are only guidelines and how much sugar you are safe to consume varies on your size and how active you are. For example, if you exercise a lot, your body may process and deal with sugar a lot better and you can get away with having more. If you're diabetic or very sedentary, you'll need to watch your sugar intake even more stringently.

How much sugar are we eating?
According to the government's National Diet and Nutrition Survey, UK adults currently eat on average 60g added sugar (and 96.5g total sugars), which is around 20 per cent too much of the harmful added type. In young people the situation is worse. In 11–18 year olds, 15 per cent of food energy is provided by sugar, which is about 50 per cent more than recommended.

Of British 11–18 year olds 2.5 per cent – that's around 50 pupils in each large senior school – get up to a third of their calories from added sugars. This is a shocking three times more than is currently deemed a healthy limit. When you consider that some authorities believe sugar recommendations in the UK to be overly lenient (see the 'New sugar guidelines' box, overleaf), it's easy to see why experts are worried about our intake and the impact on our health.

Interpreting labels
When you're trying to sleuth out the sugar in your food, it's important to be aware that it can occur under several guises. Words used to describe added sugar can include any of the following:

Sucrose
Glucose
Fructose
Maltose
Hydrolysed starch
Invert sugar
Corn syrup

It's compulsory that added sugars must be included in the ingredients list of a food and the ingredients list must start with the most prolific ingredient and work down to the least prolific. This means if you see one or more of the names above near the top of the list, you know the food you're looking at is likely to be high in added sugars.

Most supermarket foods do state the sugar content within the nutrition panel on the label, but it is not compulsory for manufacturers to do so and the figure for sugars makes no distinction between added sugars and the less worrisome types found in whole fruits and milk. If you're comparing two foods with similar amounts of total sugars, one that contains lots of fruit or milk will be a healthier choice than one that contains lots of added sugars.

Where does the sugar in our diet come from?

- **Sugar, preserves and confectionery = up to 27 per cent of our daily intake of added sugar**
  A large chunk of the added sugar in our daily diet (more than a quarter) comes from table sugar, jams, chocolate and sweets, with chocolate regularly voted Britain's favourite sweet treat.
- **Soft drinks = around 25 per cent of our daily intake of added sugar**
  Nearly a quarter of the added sugar in our diet comes from soft drinks, fruit juice and other non-alcoholic drinks. The levels are even higher among children aged 11–18 years, who get 40 per cent of their added sugar from drinks – mainly soft drinks, such as cola.
- **Biscuits, buns, cakes = 20 per cent of our daily intake of added sugar**
  The likes of pastries, muffins, buns and biscuits supply a fifth of the sugars in our diet. They're also high in fat and calories.
- **Alcoholic drinks = 11 per cent of our daily intake of added sugar**
  Booze is a surprisingly large contributor of sugar at over a tenth on average. Cutting down on alcohol and sugary mixers can have a big effect on your sugar intake and your general health too.

LIQUID SUGARS

Sugary drinks can be particularly pernicious, and have been specifically linked with obesity in children. Drinks are the largest contributor to added sugar intake for children aged 4–18. The issue is that when we drink 'liquid candy' we do not feel as full as if we had eaten the same calories from solid food and do not compensate by eating less. The bottom line? It's an easy win to drop the sugar from sugary drinks. Simply swap the full-sugar versions for low-calorie or calorie-free ones instead – better for your teeth and your waistline.

- **Dairy products = 6 per cent of our daily intake of added sugar**
  We don't need to cut down on lactose (the natural sugar in dairy), as it's not as damaging to our teeth as added sugars, plus dairy products contain lots of helpful calcium for bones. However, some dairy products, such as flavoured milks, yogurts and dairy-based desserts such as ice cream, contain added sugar, including table sugar, fructose, concentrated fruit juice and glucose-fructose syrup.
- **Savoury food = 5 per cent of our daily intake of added sugar**
  Surprisingly large amounts of sugar are found in many savoury foods, such as stir-in sauces, ketchups, salad creams, ready meals, marinades, chutneys and crisps. A 2007 study by *Which?* found some ready meals had more sugar content than vanilla ice cream.

What's a lot/little sugar?
Look for the 'carbohydrates (of which sugars)' figure on the nutrition label to see how much sugar the product contains for every 100g.
- More than 22.5g of total sugars per 100g is high (if it's a drink, more than 11.25g per 100ml).
- 5g of total sugars or less per 100g is low (if it's a drink, less than 2.5g per 100ml).
- If the amount of sugars per 100g is between these figures, the food contains a medium level of sugars.

NEW SUGAR GUIDELINES
Recently the World Health Organization (WHO) suggested that the recommended limit for added sugar consumption should ideally be halved to 5 per cent of our daily energy (calorie) consumption. That would mean having no more than about 25–35g added sugar a day – or the amount in just one large (250ml) fruit juice. According to the WHO there could be further health benefits for the general public from making these extra reductions but realistically it's a level that would be hard to stick to on a daily basis. If you're not overweight, are active and otherwise eating healthily, trying to meet this lower limit is unlikely to hold much advantage, especially compared with the effort involved.

Tips to cut down

- Instead of sugary, fizzy drinks and juice drinks, go for water or unsweetened fruit juice (remember to dilute these for children to further reduce the sugar).
- If you like fizzy drinks, try diluting fruit juice with sparkling water.
- Swap cakes or biscuits for a currant bun, scone or some malt loaf with low-fat spread.
- If you take sugar in hot drinks or add sugar to your breakfast cereal, gradually reduce the amount until you can cut it out altogether.
- Rather than spreading jam, marmalade, syrup, treacle or honey on your toast, try a low-fat spread, sliced banana or low-fat cream cheese instead.
- Check nutrition labels to help you pick the foods with less added sugar, or go for the low-sugar version.
- Try halving the sugar you use in your recipes – it works for most things except jam, meringues and ice cream.
- Choose tins of fruit in juice rather than syrup.
- Choose wholegrain breakfast cereals, but not those coated with sugar or honey.

JUDGING JUICE

Fruit juice is full of added sugars and whether it should be counted as one of our five-a-day fruit and veg has come under question. Researchers at Glasgow University found increased waist size and increased insulin resistance in overweight adults who drank grape juice daily, but the study participants downed 500ml a day – too much by any standard. If you do include fruit juice as part of your diet go back to 1970s portions and drink no more than 150ml once a day. This amount still supplies 50 per cent of your vitamin C recommended daily allowance (RDA), but a manageable 3.75 teaspoons of sugar.

Minimizing the damage

If you want to eat sugar with minimum damage to your health, here's how:

- Get exercising – studies show regular strenuous exercise like running can mean you get away with eating a lot more sugar before it causes you any harm. Indeed athletes may actually benefit from specifically choosing sugary foods – for example, as fuel during intense exercise sessions lasting 90 minutes or more.

- Eat your sugary treats with or after a meal – the impact on your teeth and blood sugar will be a lot less.
- On a similar theme, for the sake of your teeth and oral health, try to minimize the number of sugar 'hits' you get in one day – better to eat a packet of sweets in one go rather than stretched out over a few hours.
- Choose sugary foods with other redeeming qualities – sweet fruits come along with lots of fibre or vitamins, for example, while dairy products like milkshakes and dairy ice cream contain a lot of calcium.

Sugar in context

With all the media scare headlines, you might be beginning to wonder if you can ever enjoy a slice of cake or sweet treat again. But don't panic – there's absolutely no need to remove all sugar from your diet and a few sugary foods in the context of a balanced diet and lifestyle is absolutely fine.

Though the recent headlines on sugar intake look scary, our consumption hasn't recently sky rocketed, and has stayed broadly similar (with some small slight decline, in fact) since the 1980s. Consequently it's fine to make small steps towards reducing your intake rather than doing it all in one fell swoop if you don't want to. While we undoubtedly eat too much on average, no two of us are exactly the same. So when considering your own sugar intake it's important to do so in the context of your own specific lifestyle.

It's also never good to demonize just one nutrient. Saturated fat, sugar and salt are all important to consider in the context of an overall healthy diet. That's why in this book we've listed all those 'baddies' enabling you to see food in context. It's also very important not to forget that food is more than fuel – it's enjoyment too!

Sugar swapper

Sugar intake can easily mount up, but can be just as easy to reduce with a few tweaks. Here's a 'before' and 'after' example for one day, showing where tweaks can be made.

BREAKFAST

Before
40g bowl of fruit and fibre with 125ml milk (16g sugar).
200ml glass of orange juice (19.2g sugar).

After
2 Weetabix with 125ml milk (10.7g sugar).
2 small clementines (7g sugar).

MID-MORNING SNACK

Before
Cup of tea with 1 sugar and a chocolate digestive (10.6g sugar).

After
Cup of tea with no sugar and a ginger oat cake (3.4g sugar).

LUNCH

Before
Cheddar and pickle sandwich
(7.5g sugar).
Apple and can of ginger beer
(64.6g sugar).

After
Prawn sandwich with handful of
cherry tomatoes (2.4g sugar).
Apple and fizzy mineral water
(14.3g sugar).

MID-AFTERNOON SNACK

Before
30g handful raisins (20.7g sugar).

After
30g handful of roasted salted
cashews (2.6g sugar).

DINNER

Before
Chicken, veg and noodles stir-fry
with sweet chilli sauce (19.9g sugar).
125g pot of low-fat raspberry yogurt
(16.5g sugar).

After
Chicken and veg stir-fry with a
tablespoon of soy sauce (7.2g sugar).
90g bowl of raspberries with 125g of
fat-free Greek yogurt (9.1g sugar).

TOTALS

Before 175g total sugar.

After 56.7g total sugar.

Using this book

To make this book as easy to use and informative as possible, entries in each chapter are listed in logical food groups and ordered alphabetically within each group.

In the columns, you'll see that we've listed the amount of sugar per portion in grams and teaspoons (4g level teaspoons), with the average portion size accurately described where required for clarity. Note that portions will be given in either grams or mls depending on the product. As a general rule, average portion sizes are given in grams for solids and in mls for liquids. We have outlined on each page the measure that has been used for that page's products.

Be aware of average portion sizes particularly for packaged products that tend to come in a variety of sizes. Unless specified, it is safest to assume that products listed will class a small or individual-sized packet as the average portion. This particularly applies to items such as chocolate bars, bags of crisps and packets of sweets, which often come in a variety of sizes ranging from smaller individual packets to grab bags, sharing blocks and even party-sized packs. We do not anticipate that you will be doing your shopping with an accurate digital scale to hand. So always check individual wrappers and packaging for accurate product weights and use the average portion sizes given in this book as a guide where appropriate.

This book also lists sugar per 100g. This is very helpful for when your portion size might differ slightly from the average, or when you are comparing across food groups. As extra information we also list the saturated fat (saturates), energy (calorie) and salt content per 100g, giving you a feel for levels of other not-so-good components in the food. As a guide, more than 5g of saturated fat (saturates per 100g) is a lot and 1.5g or less is only a little. With salt, more than 1.5g salt per 100g is a lot and 0.3g or less is a little.

Where nutritional information is not supplied by the manufacturer you will see an *. Manufacturers are not legally required to supply the sugar, saturate or salt content of foods. While the vast majority do, there are a few times, often due to label size restrictions, where figures are omitted. In the case where you see 'trace', the amount of the nutrient in question can be considered negligible.

Seeing red

Most helpfully of all for at-a-glance use, is the green, amber and red traffic light coding system, which you may also find used on some food packaging:

- Green foods have up to 5g of sugar per 100g.
- Amber foods have between 5g and 22.5g sugar per 100g.
- Red foods have more than 22.5g sugar per 100g. A food will also be coded red if an average portion has more than 27g sugar, irrespective of the amount it contains per100g.

With drinks the coding is slightly different:

- Green drinks have up to 2.5g sugar per 100ml.
- Amber drinks have between 2.5g and 11.25g sugar per 100ml.
- Red drinks have more than 11.25g sugar per 100ml. A drink will also be coded red if an average serving has more than 13.5g sugar, irrespective of the amount per 100ml.

Please note the traffic light coding is for sugar only and some foods that score low for sugar may be high in saturates and salt or vice versa.

We've logically concentrated more on food groups that are known harbourers of sugar and lightly skimmed through foods that predominantly come out green.

We've tried to include as many popular products as possible in the space available, but if the exact brand you're after isn't listed there will usually be one very similar, or a generic item, that you can use instead. Note that unless the listed products are specified as branded or, say, value or premium, then average supermarket products/equivalent products have been featured throughout.

Eggs and fresh, unprocessed meat and fish don't contain any sugar, so we haven't listed these at all.

This book is small enough to carry around and flick through on shopping trips or days out when you may be making impromptu food purchases. Use it regularly and you'll soon get a clear picture of where the sugar in your food lies and where you can make sugar savings for the benefit of your health, waistline and wellbeing.

AN AVERAGE
PORTION EQUALS
(G):

Don't automatically reject a cereal because of the sugar content – it may still be a good option if it's high in fibre and added vitamins and minerals.

Branded cereals

All-Bran	40
All-Bran, red berry crunch	45
Blueberry wheats	50
Cheerios	30
Coco Pops	30
Coco Pops, coco rocks	30
Cookie Crisp	40
Corn flakes	30
Corn flakes, honey nut	30
Curiously Cinnamon	30
Frosted wheats	40
Frosties	30
Fruit and fibre flakes	40
Grapenuts	45
Honey Loops	30
Just Right	40
Multi-Grain Start	40
Oatibix Flakes	30
Oatibix Flakes, mixed raisin and sultana	40
Oats & More, almond	40
Oats & More, raisin	40
Optivita Berry Oat Crisp	30
Puffed wheat	30
Raisin wheats	50
Rice Krispies	30
Rice Krispies, multigrain shapes	30
Shredded wheat (2 biscuits)	45
Shreddies	40
Shreddies, coco	40
Special K	30
Special K, chocolate	30
Special K, fruit and nut	40
Special K, honey clusters	45

SUGAR PER PORTION (G)	TEASPOONS OF SUGAR PER PORTION	SUGAR PER 100G	ENERGY (KCAL) PER 100G	SATURATES PER 100G	SALT PER 100G
6.2	1.6	15.5	335	0.7	1.15
9.5	2.4	21.0	409	1.5	0.80
9.9	2.5	19.7	331	0.3	0.23
6.4	1.6	21.4	382	1.0	1.04
10.5	2.6	35.0	390	1.0	0.75
8.1	2.0	27.0	410	3.0	0.77
9.7	2.4	24.3	383	1.1	0.82
2.2	0.5	7.2	381	0.2	1.30
11.0	2.7	36.6	403	0.7	0.76
7.4	1.9	24.8	423	3.8	1.14
6.8	1.7	17.0	364	0.6	0.05
11.1	2.8	37.0	381	0.1	0.90
9.6	2.4	24.0	380	3.5	1.15
3.2	0.8	7.0	345	0.4	1.30
8.3	1.0	21.0	370	0.5	0.35
9.2	2.3	23.0	371	0.3	0.98
10.4	2.6	26.0	378	2.0	1.00
4.3	1.1	14.3	381	0.9	0.30
10.0	2.5	24.9	381	0.9	0.24
11.0	2.8	27.5	407	1.4	0.65
12.8	3.2	31.9	381	0.9	0.65
6.0	1.5	20.0	357	0.9	trace
0.2	0.0	0.6	376	0.6	trace
9.2	2.3	18.4	331	0.4	trace
3.3	0.8	10.0	391	0.2	1.15
5.4	1.4	18.0	379	0.5	0.40
0.3	0.1	0.7	363	0.5	0.05
6.0	1.5	14.9	371	0.4	0.75
11.6	2.9	28.9	375	0.7	0.63
5.1	1.3	17.0	379	0.3	1.00
7.2	1.8	24.0	398	3.5	0.55
11.2	2.8	28.0	375	0.4	0.75
10.8	2.7	24.0	392	0.9	0.60

BREAKFAST
CEREALS
AND BARS

	AN AVERAGE PORTION EQUALS (G):
Special K, oats and honey	30
Special K, red berries	30
Sugar Puffs	30
Sultana bran	40
Weetabix (2 biscuits)	37
Weetabix, banana (2 biscuits)	44
Weetabix, crunchy bran	40
Weetabix, golden syrup (2 biscuits)	44

Mueslis and granolas

Alpen, no added sugar muesli	45
Alpen, original Swiss muesli	45
Dorset Cereals granola, chocolate	45
Dorset Cereals granola, honey	45
Dorset Cereals granola, oat	45
Dorset Cereals muesli, fantastically fruity	45
Dorset Cereals muesli, luscious berries and cherries	45
Dorset Cereals muesli, simply delicious	45
Dorset Cereals muesli, simply fruity	45
Dorset Cereals muesli, simply nutty	45
Dorset Cereals muesli, tasty toasted, hazelnut and brazil	45
Dorset Cereals muesli, tasty toasted, raspberry and apple	45
Jordans country crisp cereal, chunky nuts	45
Jordans country crisp, with strawberries	45
Jordans country crisp, with tangy raspberry	45
Jordans granola, super berry	45
Jordans granola, super nutty	45

SUGAR PER PORTION (G)	TEASPOONS OF SUGAR PER PORTION	SUGAR PER 100G	ENERGY (KCAL) PER 100G	SATURATES PER 100G	SALT PER 100G
5.7	1.4	19.0	381	0.5	0.75
5.7	1.4	19.0	379	0.2	0.95
9.3	2.3	31.0	387	0.2	0.10
12.6	3.1	31.4	350	0.5	0.90
1.6	0.4	4.4	258	0.6	0.65
6.6	1.7	15.0	357	0.2	0.10
5.7	1.4	14.3	350	0.6	0.90
6.4	1.6	14.5	363	0.4	0.23
7.3	1.8	16.3	352	0.6	0.40
10.4	2.6	23.1	357	0.6	0.38
10.6	2.6	23.5	456	4.1	0.15
5.9	1.5	13.1	484	2.8	0.04
6.9	1.7	15.4	443	2.1	0.20
13.1	3.3	29.0	425	3.2	trace
16.2	4.1	36.0	332	0.3	trace
7.7	1.9	17.0	356	1.1	trace
11.7	2.9	26.0	337	0.4	trace
6.3	1.6	14.0	378	1.5	trace
6.8	1.7	15.0	409	5.5	0.40
8.6	2.1	19.0	365	0.9	0.58
9.9	2.5	21.9	492	5.4	trace
10.6	2.6	23.5	453	4.8	trace
10.3	2.6	22.9	451	4.8	trace
9.5	2.4	21.1	438	2.6	0.03
7.5	1.9	16.6	470	3.6	trace

'No added sugar' mueslis can still score red for sugar because they contain so much dried fruit. They can be healthy, but only if you go very easy on portion size.

BREAKFAST
CEREALS
AND BARS 21

	AN AVERAGE PORTION EQUALS (G):
Jordans muesli, natural	45
Muesli, 50 per cent fruit	50
Muesli, fruit and nut	50
Muesli, wholewheat	50
Pertwood organic muesli, fruit and seed	50

Porridges and oat cereals

Dorset Cereals porridge, oat and barley (1 sachet; 150ml semi-skimmed milk)	192
Dorset Cereals porridge, raspberry (1 sachet; 150ml semi-skimmed milk)	196
Oat So Simple, golden syrup (36g sachet; 180ml semi-skimmed milk)	216
Oat So Simple, original (27g sachet; 180ml semi-skimmed milk)	207
Porridge, made with water (medium bowl, no sugar)	260
Porridge, made with whole milk (medium bowl, no sugar)	260
Porridge oats	50
Pret porridge with compote topping	332
Ready Brek (without milk)	30
Ready Brek, chocolate (without milk)	30

Cereal bars

9bar, flax seed bar	40
9bar, original, seed bar	40
9bar, pumpkin bar	40
Alpen, blueberry, cranberry & yogurt cereal bar	29
Alpen, coconut & milk cereal bar	29
Alpen, fruit & nut cereal bar	28
Alpen, fruit & nut with chocolate cereal bar	29

The average portion given for each cereal bar is 1 bar.

SUGAR PER PORTION (G)	TEASPOONS OF SUGAR PER PORTION	SUGAR PER 100G	ENERGY (KCAL) PER 100G	SATURATES PER 100G	SALT PER 100G
7.0	1.8	15.6	357	0.7	0.01
16.4	4.1	32.7	378	0.4	trace
11.4	2.8	22.7	379	2.3	trace
12.1	3.0	24.2	354	2.0	trace
7.5	1.9	14.9	394	1.1	0.03
8.5	2.1	4.4	116	1.1	0.05
13.1	3.3	6.7	139	1.3	0.10
15.9	4.0	7.4	100	1.1	0.19
8.4	2.1	4.1	87	1.1	0.10
0.3	0.1	0.1	46	0.2	trace
12.5	3.1	4.8	113	2.8	trace
0.5	0.1	1.0	370	1.2	trace
13.9	3.5	4.2	83	1.4	trace
0.3	0.1	1.0	373	1.2	trace
6.3	1.6	21.0	380	2.2	0.03
12.0	3.0	30.0	523	10.0	trace
10.5	2.6	26.2	555	10.1	trace
9.4	2.4	23.5	510	6.6	trace
10.1	2.5	34.9	422	6.3	0.15
8.1	2.0	28.0	432	0.2	
8.9	2.2	31.8	389	1.5	0.28
10.5	2.6	36.1	425	5.1	0.20

Pick your cereal bar carefully – they may be a bit better than chocolate, but almost all of them are high sugar. Look for those that are high fibre, too.

	AN AVERAGE PORTION EQUALS (G):
Alpen Light, sultana & apple cereal bar	19
Alpen Light, summer fruit cereal bar	19
Alpen, raspberry & yogurt cereal bar	29
Alpen, strawberry & yogurt cereal bar	29
Brunch bar, choc chip	32
Brunch bar, hazelnut	32
Brunch bar, raisin	32
Coco Pops cereal & milk bar	20
Dorset Cereal bar, date & pecan	40
Eat Natural fruits and fibre bar, apricot & coconut	40
Eat Natural fruits and fibre bar, peanut & plum	40
Frosties snack bar	25
Fruitus, apricot oat bar	35
Fruitus, mixed berry oat bar	35
Go Ahead yogurt break, forest fruit (1 slice)	36
Go Ahead yogurt break, strawberry (1 slice)	36
Jordan's absolute berry bar	45
Jordans absolute nut bar	45
Jordan's crunchy cereal bar, honey & almond	30
Jordans frusli bar, blueberry burst	30
Jordans frusli bar, cranberry & apple	30
Jordans frusli bar, juicy apples & sultanas	30
Jordans frusli bar, raisin & hazelnut	30
Jordans frusli bar, wild berries	30
Näkd berry delight bar	35
Näkd cocoa delight bar	35

SUGAR PER PORTION (G)	TEASPOONS OF SUGAR PER PORTION	SUGAR PER 100G	ENERGY (KCAL) PER 100G	SATURATES PER 100G	SALT PER 100G
4.7	1.2	24.5	330	1.5	0.18
4.3	1.1	22.8	334	1.5	0.20
10.6	2.7	36.6	419	6.1	0.19
10.0	2.5	34.6	412	1.6	0.05
12.4	3.1	38.8	445	9.0	0.63
11.8	2.9	36.8	470	8.5	0.57
13.6	3.4	42.5	430	8.1	0.58
8.4	2.1	42.0	415	9.0	0.50
12.4	3.1	31.0	452	3.5	trace
12.8	3.2	31.9	419	8.6	trace
9.5	2.4	23.7	441	0.4	trace
8.0	2.0	32.0	414	7.0	0.75
11.6	2.9	33.2	370	2.8	trace
12.4	3.1	35.4	392	3.2	trace
14.4	3.6	40.7	418	4.6	0.50
7.3	1.8	41.2	417	4.6	0.50
17.9	4.5	39.8	370	1.2	trace
7.2	1.8	15.9	578	3.9	trace
6.7	1.7	22.2	445	1.6	0.12
9.9	2.5	33.1	375	1.4	trace
10.4	2.6	34.7	376	1.4	trace
10.8	2.7	36.1	369	1.7	trace
6.6	1.7	32.1	390	1.8	trace
10.1	2.5	33.8	374	1.5	0.25
16.0	4.0	47.0	385	3.0	trace
15.0	3.8	45.0	386	3.0	trace

BREAKFAST
CEREALS
AND BARS 25

	AN AVERAGE PORTION EQUALS (G):
Nākd cocoa orange bar	35
Nākd strawberry crunch bar	30
Nature Valley crunchy bar, Canadian maple syrup	42
Nature Valley crunchy bar, cinnamon	42
Nature Valley crunchy bar, oats & chocolate	42
Nature Valley crunchy bar, oats & honey	42
Nutri-Grain crunchy oat granola bar, cinnamon	40
Nutri-Grain crunchy oat granola bar, honey	40
Rice Krispies cereal & milk bar	20
Rice Krispies squares, marshmallow	28
Special K bar, chocolate & raspberry	22
Special K biscuit moments, raspberry	25
Special K chewy delight bar, dark chocolate	24
Special K chewy delight bar, milk chocolate	24
Special K multigrain red berry bar	27
Special K peach & apricot bar	23
Tracker, chocolate chip	37
Tracker, crunchy peanut	37
Tracker, roast nut	26
Tracker, white chocolate chip	26
Weetabix oaty bar, milk chocolate	23
Weetabix oaty bar, toffee	23

Breakfast bars and biscuits

9bar breakfast, apricot and strawberry	50
All-Bran breakfast biscuits, chocolate (4 biscuits)	40

SUGAR PER PORTION (G)	TEASPOONS OF SUGAR PER PORTION	SUGAR PER 100G	ENERGY (KCAL) PER 100G	SATURATES PER 100G	SALT PER 100G
14.0	3.5	39.0	415	4.0	trace
13.0	3.3	43.4	362	1.8	0.20
11.8	3.0	28.0	457	2.7	0.70
11.0	2.8	26.1	472	3.2	0.90
11.7	2.9	27.9	466	5.3	0.60
11.9	3.0	28.3	456	2.4	0.80
9.0	2.3	22.0	465	2.5	0.93
11.0	2.8	29.0	436	2.0	0.85
7.0	1.8	35.0	413	8.0	0.65
9.0	2.2	32.0	406	5.0	0.75
8.0	2.0	16.0	411	5.0	0.65
7.5	1.9	30.0	383	3.4	0.88
5.0	1.3	20.0	404	6.0	0.35
6.0	1.5	24.0	397	5.0	0.43
3.5	0.9	13.0	385	0.8	0.08
8.0	2.0	34.0	389	4.0	0.63
11.3	2.8	30.6	483	10.2	0.43
10.4	2.6	28.0	489	9.5	0.43
7.3	1.8	28.0	489	9.5	0.43
8.4	2.1	32.4	482	10.0	0.45
3.6	0.9	15.5	342	2.1	0.21
4.5	1.1	19.6	348	2.9	0.21
15.0	3.7	29.9	451	5.2	0.64
9.2	2.3	23.0	418	5.0	0.50

	AN AVERAGE PORTION EQUALS (G):
Belvita breakfast biscuits, honey & nuts (1 pack/4 biscuits)	50
Belvita breakfast biscuits, milk & cereals (1 pack/4 biscuits)	50
Belvita duo crunch, strawberry & live yogurt (1 pack/2 biscuits)	50
Jordans breakfast bar, cranberry & raspberry	40
Jordans breakfast bar, fruit & nut	40
Jordans breakfast bar, maple & pecan	40
McVitie's breakfast biscuits, raspberry & yogurt	51
Nutri-Grain breakfast biscuits, cereal & milk (1 pack/4 biscuits)	44
Nutri-Grain breakfast biscuits, chocolate (1 pack/4 biscuits)	44
Nutri-Grain breakfast biscuits, fruit & fibre (1 pack/4 biscuits)	44
Nutri-Grain Elevenses, raisin bakes	45
Oats So Simple morning bar, fruit muesli	35
Oat So Simple morning bar, golden syrup	35
Oats So Simple oats & milk breakfast biscuits (4 biscuits)	40
Weetabix breakfast biscuits, apple & cinnamon	50
Weetabix breakfast biscuits, fruit & fibre	50
Weetabix breakfast biscuits, milk & cereals	50

SUGAR PER PORTION (G)	TEASPOONS OF SUGAR PER PORTION	SUGAR PER 100G	ENERGY (KCAL) PER 100G	SATURATES PER 100G	SALT PER 100G
13.5	3.4	27.0	450	1.7	0.90
10.0	2.5	20.0	440	1.4	0.98
13.2	3.3	26.0	445	2.9	0.57
13.8	3.5	34.6	370	1.2	trace
12.4	3.1	31.0	411	2.7	trace
11.2	2.8	27.9	388	1.5	trace
13.2	3.3	25.7	487	9.3	0.70
6.0	1.5	14.0	429	4.0	0.58
11.0	2.8	24.0	446	4.0	0.45
8.0	2.0	18.0	429	4.0	0.48
16.0	4.0	36.0	398	3.5	0.50
6.5	1.6	18.7	398	2.7	0.46
5.4	1.3	15.4	407	3.0	0.51
6.8	1.7	17.0	430	4.0	1.09
7.8	2.0	15.6	440	4.3	0.42
9.7	2.4	19.3	437	4.0	0.43
7.3	1.8	14.5	438	4.0	0.43

	AN AVERAGE PORTION EQUALS (G):
Vegetables	
Aduki beans, boiled (3 tbsp)	120
Asparagus, raw (5 spears)	125
Aubergines, raw	80
Beetroot, boiled (2 small)	70
Beetroot, pickled in jar	50
Blackeye beans, boiled (3 tbsp)	120
Broad beans, boiled (2 tbsp)	120
Broccoli, raw	80
Brussels sprouts, raw (9 sprouts)	90
Butter beans, canned in water (4 tbsp)	120
Butternut squash, flesh	160
Cabbage, raw	95
Carrot and swede mash, frozen, cooked	160
Carrots, raw (1 medium)	80
Cauliflower, raw	90
Celery (1 stalk)	60
Chickpeas, canned in water (4 tbsp)	120
Chilli (1 chilli)	20
Courgettes, raw (1 medium)	150
Cucumber (2.5 cm piece)	60
Fennel	80
Garlic (1 clove)	3
Green beans, raw	80
Kale, raw	80
Leeks, raw (1 medium)	160
Lentils, boiled (4 tbsp)	20
Lettuce, Cos	80
Lettuce iceberg	80
Lettuce, round	80
Mangetout, raw	80
Mung beansprouts, raw (4 tbsp)	80
Mushrooms, raw, all types	80

SUGAR PER PORTION (G)	TEASPOONS OF SUGAR PER PORTION	SUGAR PER 100G	ENERGY (KCAL) PER 100G	SATURATES PER 100G	SALT PER 100G
0.6	0.2	0.5	123	trace	trace
2.4	0.6	1.9	25	0.1	trace
1.6	0.4	2.0	15	0.1	trace
6.2	1.5	8.8	46	trace	trace
2.9	0.7	5.8	38	0.0	0.80
1.3	0.3	1.1	116	0.2	trace
1.6	0.4	1.3	81	0.1	trace
1.2	0.3	1.5	33	0.2	trace
2.8	0.7	3.1	42	0.3	trace
0.4	0.1	0.3	77	0.1	trace
5.9	1.5	3.7	41	0.0	trace
3.8	1.0	4.0	26	0.1	trace
6.0	1.5	3.8	45	1.4	0.70
5.9	1.5	7.4	35	0.1	trace
2.3	0.6	2.5	34	0.2	trace
0.5	0.1	0.9	7	trace	0.10
0.6	0.2	0.5	109	0.4	trace
0.1	0.0	0.7	20	*	trace
2.7	0.7	1.8	18	0.1	trace
0.8	0.2	1.4	10	trace	trace
1.4	0.3	1.7	12	trace	trace
trace	trace	1.6	98	trace	trace
1.8	0.5	2.3	24	0.1	trace
1.0	0.3	1.3	33	trace	trace
3.5	0.9	2.2	22	0.1	trace
1.0	0.2	0.8	100	trace	trace
1.4	0.3	1.7	16	trace	trace
1.5	0.4	1.9	13	trace	trace
0.8	0.2	1.0	12	trace	trace
2.7	0.7	3.4	32	trace	trace
1.8	0.4	2.2	31	0.1	trace
0.1	0.0	0.2	13	0.1	trace

As well as being filling, low calorie and full of fibre and vitamins, vegetables are generally very low in sugar. We should aim to eat more of them than fruit.

VEGETABLES AND SALAD

	AN AVERAGE PORTION EQUALS (G):
Mushy peas, canned (½ can)	150
Okra, raw	80
Onions, peeled, raw (½ medium)	75
Parsnips, raw (1 medium)	90
Peas, frozen, boiled	80
Peas, raw, shelled	80
Peppers, green (½ medium)	80
Peppers, red (½ medium)	80
Petit pois, frozen, boiled	80
Pickled gherkins, drained (1 gherkin)	40
Plantain, fried in vegetable oil	100
Potatoes, baked, flesh and skin (1 medium)	180
Potatoes, new, raw (3 potatoes)	120
Potatoes, old, raw (2 potatoes)	120
Pumpkin, flesh, raw	160
Raddicchio	80
Radishes (4 radishes)	32
Shallots, peeled, raw (1 shallot)	40
Spinach, raw	90
Spring greens, raw	90
Spring onions (4 spring onions)	40
Swede, raw	80
Sweet potatoes, flesh	30
Sweetcorn, canned, no sugar or salt (3 rounded tbsp)	80
Tomatoes, raw (1 medium)	85
Turnip, boiled (1 medium)	110
Watercress	80
Yam, raw	130

Prepared salad

Bean salad (½ pot)	112
Caesar salad kit (½ pack)	132

SUGAR PER PORTION (G)	TEASPOONS OF SUGAR PER PORTION	SUGAR PER 100G	ENERGY (KCAL) PER 100G	SATURATES PER 100G	SALT PER 100G
1.4	0.3	0.9	69	trace	0.35
2.0	0.5	2.5	31	0.3	trace
4.2	1.1	5.6	36	trace	trace
5.1	1.3	5.7	64	0.2	trace
2.2	0.5	2.7	69	0.2	trace
1.8	0.5	2.3	83	0.3	trace
1.9	0.5	2.4	15	0.1	trace
4.9	1.2	6.1	32	0.1	trace
2.4	0.6	3.0	49	0.2	trace
2.2	0.6	5.5	31	trace	1.30
11.5	2.9	11.5	267	1.0	trace
2.2	0.5	1.2	136	trace	trace
1.6	0.4	1.3	70	0.1	trace
0.7	0.2	0.6	75	trace	trace
2.7	0.7	1.7	55	0.1	trace
1.30	0.3	1.7	14	trace	trace
0.6	0.2	1.9	49	trace	trace
1.2	0.3	3.1	86	0.1	trace
1.4	0.3	1.5	25	0.1	trace
2.4	0.6	2.7	33	0.1	trace
1.1	0.3	2.8	23	0.1	trace
3.9	1.0	4.9	24	trace	trace
7.4	1.9	5.7	87	0.1	trace
3.6	0.9	4.5	73	0.3	trace
2.6	0.7	3.1	17	0.1	trace
2.1	0.5	1.9	12	trace	trace
0.3	0.1	0.4	22	0.3	trace
0.9	0.2	0.7	114	0.1	trace
1.1	0.3	1.0	107	0.4	0.25
3.0	0.8	2.3	168	1.8	0.57

	AN AVERAGE PORTION EQUALS (G):
Caesar salad kit, reduced fat (½ pack)	132
Classic salad bowl	84
Coleslaw (2 heaped tbsp)	75
Coleslaw, premium (2 heaped tbsp)	75
Coleslaw, reduced fat (2 heaped tbsp)	75
Edamame salad with chilli and coriander dressing (½ pot)	93
Greek salad	200
Pasta salad, spinach and pine nut	150
Pasta salad, tomato and basil	150
Potato salad (2 heaped tbsp)	75
Sweet and crispy salad bowl (with mayo)	125
Tuna nicoise salad	280

Chips and prepared potato products

Aunt Bessie's Home-style roast potatoes, baked	150
Aunt Bessie's roasting carrots	80
Aunt Bessie's roasting parsnips	80
Aunt Bessie's special vegetable mash	160
Chips, chip shop, fried in vegetable oil (no salt and vinegar)	210
Chips, oven, baked	150
Croquettes, baked	2 croquettes
Mashed potato	200
Mashed potato with Cheddar	225
McCain hash browns, baked	100
McCain Micro Chips, cooked (1 box)	88
McCain Smiles	100
McCain southern fries, baked	100
Potato waffles, baked (1 waffle)	56
Wedges, spiced or flavoured	150

SUGAR PER PORTION (G)	TEASPOONS OF SUGAR PER PORTION	SUGAR PER 100G	ENERGY (KCAL) PER 100G	SATURATES PER 100G	SALT PER 100G
2.9	0.7	2.2	108	1.2	0.50
1.9	0.5	2.3	21	trace	0.10
3.4	0.8	4.5	181	1.9	0.75
4.1	1.0	5.4	238	2.7	0.78
4.4	1.1	5.9	100	0.7	0.65
4.8	1.2	5.2	121	0.7	0.38
6.0	1.5	3.0	122	3.6	0.25
1.8	0.5	1.2	231	2.9	1.00
8.1	2.0	5.4	147	0.7	0.98
0.9	0.2	1.2	140	1.5	0.43
3.5	0.9	3.2	124	0.9	0.23
6.2	2.2	2.2	92	0.7	0.33
0.9	0.2	0.6	167	2.7	0.50
5.8	1.5	7.3	100	0.8	0.68
5.4	1.4	6.8	196	5.6	0.30
6.0	1.5	3.8	45	1.4	0.70
1.5	0.4	0.7	364	4.0	0.25
0.9	0.2	0.6	158	0.4	0.10
1.5	0.4	2.1	223	1.4	0.46
2.2	0.6	1.1	69	1.0	0.25
2.0	0.5	0.9	127	4.5	0.53
0.5	0.1	0.5	170	0.7	1.00
0.4	0.1	0.5	185	0.6	0.30
0.8	0.2	0.8	213	1.0	0.20
0.6	0.2	0.6	222	0.9	0.70
trace	0.0	trace	234	1.2	0.50
0.9	0.2	0.6	187	0.8	0.80

VEGETABLES
AND SALAD 35

Grapes are one of the highest sugar fruits, so why not weigh a handful before you tuck in to avoid overindulging?

	AN AVERAGE PORTION EQUALS (G):
Fresh and dried fruit	
Apples, cooking, raw, peeled, without core (1 medium)	130
Apples, cooking, stewed with sugar	110
Apples, cooking, stewed without sugar	110
Apples, eating, with skin, without core (1 medium)	100
Apricots, canned in juice (¼ can)	104
Apricots, canned in syrup (¼ can)	104
Apricots, dried (4 dried apricots)	32
Apricots, fresh, no stones (2 apricots)	80
Avocado, flesh (1 medium)	145
Bananas, no skin (1 medium)	95
Blackberries	80
Blueberries	80
Cherries, no stones (20 cherries)	80
Clementines, without skin (2 small)	80
Cranberries, dried	30
Currants (1 heaped tbsp)	25
Damsons, raw, no stones (4 damsons)	60
Damsons, stewed with sugar	110
Dates, dried, no stones (2 dates)	30
Dried mixed fruit (1 heaped tbsp)	25
Figs, dried (1 dried fig)	20
Figs, raw (1 medium)	55
Fruit cocktail, canned in juice (¼ can)	104
Fruit cocktail, canned in syrup (¼ can)	104
Fruit salad, home made	140
Glacé cherries	25
Gooseberries, cooking, raw	80
Gooseberries, stewed with sugar	140
Grapefruit, canned in juice (¼ can)	135
Grapefruit, canned in syrup (¼ can)	135
Grapefruit, flesh (½ grapefruit)	80

Where fruit is outlined as 'stewed with sugar', the recipe that has been used is 1kg fruit with 120g sugar, simmered in a little water.

SUGAR PER PORTION (G)	TEASPOONS OF SUGAR PER PORTION	SUGAR PER 100G	ENERGY (KCAL) PER 100G	SATURATES PER 100G	SALT PER 100G
11.6	2.9	8.9	35	trace	trace
21.0	5.3	19.1	74	trace	trace
8.9	2.2	8.1	33	trace	trace
11.8	3.0	11.8	47	trace	trace
8.7	2.2	8.4	34	trace	trace
16.7	4.2	16.1	63	trace	trace
13.9	3.5	43.4	188	trace	trace
5.8	1.4	7.2	31	trace	trace
0.7	0.2	0.5	190	4.1	trace
19.9	5.0	20.9	95	0.1	trace
4.1	1.0	5.1	25	trace	trace
8.0	2.0	10.0	69	trace	trace
9.2	2.3	11.5	48	trace	trace
7.0	1.7	8.7	37	trace	trace
19.5	4.9	65.0	335	0.1	trace
17.0	4.2	67.8	267	trace	trace
5.8	1.4	9.6	38	trace	trace
21.2	5.3	19.3	74	trace	trace
20.4	5.1	68.0	270	0.1	trace
17.0	4.3	68.1	268	trace	0.10
10.6	2.6	52.9	227	trace	0.10
5.2	1.3	9.5	43	trace	trace
7.5	1.9	7.2	29	trace	trace
15.4	3.8	14.8	57	trace	trace
20.2	5.0	14.4	60	trace	trace
16.6	4.2	66.4	251	trace	trace
2.4	0.6	3.0	19	trace	trace
18.1	4.5	12.9	54	trace	trace
9.9	2.5	7.3	30	trace	trace
20.9	5.2	15.5	60	trace	trace
5.4	1.4	6.8	30	trace	trace

Obviously, the greater the sugar : fruit ratio, the higher the sugar content of the stewed fruit.

	AN AVERAGE PORTION EQUALS (G):
Grapes (small bunch)	100
Kiwi fruit, flesh (1 medium)	60
Lemons (1 slice)	20
Loganberries	80
Lychees, flesh, no stone	60
Mandarins, canned in juice (½ can)	150
Mandarins, canned in syrup (½ can)	150
Mango, dried	30
Mango, flesh (½ mango)	115
Melon, cantaloupe, flesh (1 slice)	150
Melon, Galia, flesh (1 slice)	150
Melon, honeydew, flesh (1 slice)	200
Nectarine, no stone (1 nectarine)	130
Oranges, flesh (1 medium)	160
Papaya, flesh (1 slice)	140
Passion fruit, flesh and seeds (1 medium)	15
Peach, no stone (1 medium)	130
Pears, canned in juice (¼ can)	104
Pears, canned in syrup (¼ can)	104
Pears, raw, without core (1 medium)	150
Pineapple, flesh, fresh (1 ring)	80
Pineapple, canned in juice (¼ can)	108
Pineapple, canned in syrup (¼ can)	108
Plums, no stone (1 medium)	55
Prunes, canned in juice (¼ can)	104
Prunes, canned in syrup (¼ can)	104
Prunes, semi-dried (3 prunes)	36
Raisins (1 heaped tbsp)	25
Raspberries	90
Rhubarb, stewed with sugar	140
Satsumas, flesh (1 medium)	70
Strawberries	100
Sultanas (1 heaped tbsp)	25
Watermelon, flesh (1 slice)	200

Fruit portion sizes (ie 1 slice or ½ fruit) are based on averages.
Opinions of what constitutes an appropriate portion, and the sizes

SUGAR PER PORTION (G)	TEASPOONS OF SUGAR PER PORTION	SUGAR PER 100G	ENERGY (KCAL) PER 100G	SATURATES PER 100G	SALT PER 100G
15.4	3.9	15.4	60	trace	trace
6.2	1.5	10.3	60	trace	trace
0.6	0.2	3.2	19	trace	trace
2.7	0.7	3.4	17	trace	trace
8.6	2.1	14.3	58	trace	trace
11.6	2.9	7.7	32	trace	trace
20.1	5.0	13.4	52	trace	trace
17.1	4.3	57.0	296	0.1	0.30
15.9	4.0	13.8	57	trace	trace
6.3	1.6	4.2	19	trace	trace
8.4	2.1	5.6	24	trace	0.10
13.2	3.3	6.6	28	trace	0.10
11.7	2.9	9.0	40	trace	trace
13.6	3.4	8.5	37	trace	trace
12.3	3.1	8.8	36	trace	trace
0.9	0.2	5.8	36	trace	trace
9.9	2.5	7.6	33	trace	trace
8.8	2.2	8.5	33	trace	trace
13.7	3.4	13.2	50	trace	trace
15.0	3.8	10.0	40	trace	trace
8.1	2.0	10.1	41	trace	trace
13.2	3.3	12.2	47	trace	trace
17.8	4.5	16.5	64	trace	trace
4.8	1.2	8.8	36	trace	trace
20.5	5.1	19.7	79	trace	trace
23.9	6.0	23.0	90	trace	trace
12.2	3.1	34.0	141	trace	trace
17.3	4.3	69.3	272	trace	trace
4.1	1.0	4.6	25	0.1	0.10
16.1	4.0	11.5	48	trace	trace
6.0	1.5	8.5	36	trace	trace
6.0	1.5	6.0	27	trace	trace
17.4	4.3	69.4	275	trace	trace
14.2	3.6	7.1	31	trace	trace

Choosing canned fruit in juice, rather than syrup, can lower your sugar intake considerably.

of fruit, will vary. For accurate portion sizes, weigh fruit (whole or sliced) rather than estimate.

SAUCES,
DRESSINGS
AND GRAVIES

'Sweet and sour' and
'sweet chilli' aren't
called this for nothing
– they generally have a
lot of sugar!

AN AVERAGE
PORTION EQUALS
(G):

General cooking sauces

Balti	150
Beef in ale	125
Bhuna	150
Cheese	150
Chilli con carne	125
Cottage pie cooking	125
Creamy mushroom	115
Green Thai	150
Honey mustard	125
Korma	150
Spanish chicken	125
Sweet and sour	125
Tikka masala	150

Pasta sauces

Bolognese	150
Carbonara	150
Carbonara, fresh	187
Onion and garlic	125
Pesto, classic basil	48
Pesto, red	48
Red lasagne	125
Sun dried tomato, stir-in	75
Sweet pepper, stir-in	75
Tomato and basil	150
Tomato and basil, fresh	187
Tomato and mascarpone, fresh	187
White lasagne	118

Stir-fry sauces

Black bean	90
Chinese	90
Coconut, chilli and lemongrass	90

SUGAR PER PORTION (G)	TEASPOONS OF SUGAR PER PORTION	SUGAR PER 100G	ENERGY (KCAL) PER 100G	SATURATES PER 100G	SALT PER 100G
8.7	2.2	5.8	76	0.3	0.60
7.0	1.8	5.6	46	0.1	0.70
5.7	1.4	3.8	85	0.5	0.80
3.0	0.8	2.0	124	5.6	0.68
8.6	2.2	6.9	69	trace	0.70
5.3	1.3	4.2	41	trace	0.70
1.8	0.5	1.6	80	3.7	0.80
6.2	1.5	4.1	140	7.6	0.70
20.6	5.2	16.5	86	1.0	0.70
10.1	2.5	6.7	174	8.0	0.75
8.5	2.1	6.8	55	0.2	0.60
21.9	5.5	17.5	94	trace	0.70
8.4	2.1	5.6	125	4.6	0.80
7.0	1.8	5.2	55	0.1	0.80
trace	0.0	trace	135	4.1	0.90
2.2	0.6	1.2	211	4.8	0.80
8.4	2.1	6.7	41	0.1	0.63
1.4	0.4	3.2	477	6.8	2.90
2.3	0.6	4.9	312	4.2	2.90
8.3	2.1	6.6	31	0.1	0.80
3.9	1.0	5.2	125	1.1	1.48
4.6	1.2	6.1	103	0.8	1.23
6.9	1.7	10.3	40	0.4	0.80
5.0	1.3	9.4	47	0.2	0.50
5.9	1.5	3.9	110	3.9	0.80
2.4	0.6	2.0	104	2.9	0.70
7.7	1.9	8.8	105	0.4	1.70
10.2	2.6	11.4	100	0.2	1.70
8.3	2.1	9.3	130	3.5	1.10

	AN AVERAGE PORTION EQUALS (G/ML):
Discovery medium fajita stir-in sauce	25
Discovery mild fajita stir-in sauce	25
Plum	90
Sweet and sour	90
Sweet chilli	90
Teriyaki	90

Pastes and purées

Chipotle paste	25
Curry paste, (1 tbsp)	15
Jerk paste	25
Tahini (sesame seed) paste (1 tbsp)	20
Tomato purée (1 tbsp)	15

Table sauces

Barbecue sauce (1 tbsp)	15
Blue Dragon sweet chilli dipping sauce (1 tbsp)	15ml
Branston pickle (1 tbsp)	15
Bread sauce	45
English Provender Co. apple, pear and fig chutney (1 tbsp)	15
Geeta's Lime and chilli chutney (1 tbsp)	15
Heinz, organic ketchup (1 tbsp)	17
Heinz, salad cream (1 tbsp)	15
Ketchup (1 tbsp)	17
Mango chutney (1 tbsp)	15
Mayonnaise (1 tbsp)	15
Mayonnaise, full fat (1 tbsp)	14
Piccalilli (1 tbsp)	15
Soy sauce, dark (1 tsp)	5ml
Soy sauce, light (1 tsp)	5ml
Worcestershire sauce (1 tsp)	5ml

SUGAR PER PORTION (G)	TEASPOONS OF SUGAR PER PORTION	SUGAR PER 100G/ML	ENERGY (KCAL) PER 100G/ML	SATURATES PER 100G/ML	SALT PER 100G/ML
1.7	0.4	6.6	148	0.6	1.35
2.0	0.5	7.8	156	0.7	1.18
33.6	8.4	37.3	178	trace	1.00
25.7	6.4	28.6	147	0.2	1.50
16.3	4.1	18.1	119	0.2	1.20
16.8	4.2	18.7	141	0.7	1.50
2.0	0.5	7.8	156	0.7	1.18
0.2	0.1	1.6	296	1.8	3.40
2.1	0.5	8.3	180	0.8	2.40
0.1	0.0	0.4	607	8.4	1.33
2.7	0.7	18.1	100	trace	0.50
2.8	0.7	18.4	150	trace	1.30
8.2	2.1	54.7	229	0.0	4.30
3.6	0.9	24.0	112	0.0	4.00
1.4	0.1	3.2	00	0.8	0.82
6.2	1.6	41.5	181	0.1	1.15
10.1	2.5	50.4	249	trace	4.60
4.6	1.1	27.0	119	trace	2.20
2.6	0.7	17.5	336	2.0	1.70
4.0	1.0	23.7	103	trace	2.20
8.6	2.1	57.2	239	0.4	2.40
0.3	0.1	2.2	297	3.0	2.30
0.2	0.0	1.3	722	6.6	1.50
1.2	0.3	8.0	57	trace	2.00
1.2	0.0	23.2	117	0.0	12.68
0.8	0.0	15.4	69	0.0	11.48
1.0	0.0	19.6	113	trace	3.60

Ketchup is a good source of lycopene – an antioxidant – but go easy, there's often a teaspoon of sugar in every tablespoon.

SAUCES, DRESSINGS AND GRAVIES

SAUCES,
DRESSINGS
AND GRAVIES

**AN AVERAGE
PORTION EQUALS
(ML):**

Salad dressings

Balsamic (1 tbsp)	15
Caesar, full fat, fresh (1 tbsp)	15
Caesar, light (1 tbsp)	15
French, fresh (1 tbsp)	15
French, reduced fat (1 tbsp)	15
Hellmann's garlic and herb dressing (1 tbsp)	15
Mango and chilli (1 tbsp)	15
Newman's Own, ranch (1 tbsp)	15
Pizza Express, basil pesto (1 tbsp)	15
Pizza Express, honey and mustard (1 tbsp)	15
Righteous English blue cheese and cider dressing (1 tbsp)	15
Righteous oil-free caper and peppercorn dressing (1 tbsp)	15
Righteous ginger and toasted sesame (1 tbsp)	15
Soy chilli and ginger (1 tbsp)	15
Thousand island (1 tbsp)	15

Stocks and gravies

Gravy granules, made up	50
Knorr stock pot gel, beef (¼ pot made up)	125
Knorr stock pot gel, chicken (¼ pot made up)	125
Knorr stock pot gel, rich beef (¼ pot made up)	125
Knorr stock pot gel, vegetable (¼ pot made up)	125
Stock cube, meat, made up	100
Stock cube, meat, reduced salt	100
Stock cube, vegetable, made up	100

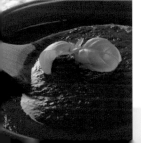

SUGAR PER PORTION (G)	TEASPOONS OF SUGAR PER PORTION	SUGAR PER 100ML	ENERGY (KCAL) PER 100ML	SATURATES PER 100ML	SALT PER 100ML
2.6	0.6	17.1	140	0.4	1.25
0.1	0.0	0.6	481	4.3	1.25
0.7	0.2	4.5	62	0.5	1.37
1.0	0.2	6.6	430	3.8	1.50
0.9	0.2	5.8	39	0.1	0.77
1.0	0.3	6.4	177	1.2	2.00
1.9	0.5	12.9	257	2.2	0.73
0.7	0.2	4.9	416	3.1	2.25
1.1	0.3	7.1	445	3.8	1.40
2.4	0.6	16.3	416	2.6	2.10
0.4	0.1	2.6	360	7.3	1.67
0.8	0.2	5.3	53	0.1	trace
1.7	0.4	11.3	440	3.3	trace
1.4	0.3	9.1	149	0.7	1.48
1.7	0.4	11.5	239	3.0	2.00
0.8	0.2	1.6	26	0.4	0.86
0.3	0.1	0.2	11	trace	0.88
0.6	0.2	0.5	12	trace	0.80
0.4	0.1	0.3	12	trace	0.80
0.4	0.1	0.3	12	trace	0.88
0.1	0.0	0.1	7	0.1	0.83
0.2	0.1	0.2	8	0.1	0.60
0.2	0.1	0.2	7	0.1	0.98

SAUCES, DRESSINGS AND GRAVIES

	AN AVERAGE PORTION EQUALS (G):
Sugars, syrups and treacle	
Silver Spoon, half spoon (½ tsp)	2
Sugar, brown (1 tsp)	4
Sugar, demerara (1 tsp)	4
Sugar, icing (1 tsp)	4
Sugar, white (1 tsp)	4
Syrup, golden (1 tbsp)	20
Syrup, maple (1 tbsp)	20
Treacle, black (1 tbsp)	20
Sweet spreads	
Chocolate spread (1 heaped tsp)	15
Galaxy hazelnut chocolate spread (1 heaped tsp)	15
Hartley's Best, apricot jam (1 heaped tsp)	15
Hartley's Best, strawberry jam (1 heaped tsp)	15
Hazelnut chocolate spread (1 heaped tsp)	15
Honey (1 level tsp)	7
Jam, fruit, seeded	15
Jam, reduced sugar	15
Jam, stone fruit	15
Lemon curd	15
Marmalade	15
Meridian almond butter (1 tbsp)	20
Milky Way chocolate spread (1 heaped tsp)	15
Nutella hazelnut chocolate spread (1 heaped tsp)	15
Peanut butter, smooth or crunchy (1 tbsp)	20
St Dalfour, fruit spread, apricot (1 rounded tsp)	15

SUGAR PER PORTION (G)	TEASPOONS OF SUGAR PER PORTION	SUGAR PER 100G	ENERGY (KCAL) PER 100G	SATURATES PER 100G	SALT PER 100G
2.0	0.5	99.0	400	0.0	0.00
4.0	1.0	99.0	399	trace	trace
3.9	1.0	98.7	397	trace	trace
4.0	1.0	99.0	399	trace	trace
4.0	1.0	99.0	325	trace	trace
16.1	4.0	80.5	325	trace	trace
12.3	3.1	61.5	254	trace	0.10
12.8	3.2	64.0	290	0.0	0.30
9.0	2.3	60.0	560	6.6	0.11
8.6	2.1	57.1	553	7.5	0.15
8.3	2.1	55.3	244	0.0	0.1
8.0	2.0	53.1	247	0.1	0.1
8.3	2.1	55.0	556	6.8	0.12
5.7	1.4	81.9	350	0	trace
10.4	2.6	69.0	261	0.0	0.07
4.8	1.2	31.9	123	0.0	0.05
10.4	2.6	69.3	261	0.0	0.12
7.7	1.9	51.3	254	1.8	0.15
10.4	2.6	69.0	261	0.0	0.15
0.8	0.2	4.0	650	4.4	0.50
8.4	2.1	56.0	559	8.2	0.25
8.5	2.1	56.7	544	10.9	0.11
0.8	0.2	3.9	620	9.3	0.70
7.8	2.0	52.0	211	0.1	trace

SYRUPS, SUGARS AND SPREADS

	AN AVERAGE PORTION EQUALS (G):
St Dalfour, fruit spread, orange & ginger (1 rounded tsp)	15
St Dalfour, fruit spread, raspberry (1 rounded tsp)	15
St Dalfour, fruit spread, strawberry (1 rounded tsp)	15
St Dalfour, fruit spread, wild blueberry (1 rounded tsp)	15
Sunpat choc-a-nut (1 tbsp)	20
Tiptree lemon curd (1 rounded tsp)	15

Savoury spreads

Beef paste (1 tbsp)	17
Cashew butter, Meridian (1 tbsp)	20
Chicken paste (1 tbsp)	17
Fluff marshmallow spread	12
Heinz Light sandwich spread (1 dessertspoon)	10
Heinz Original sandwich spread (1 dessertspoon)	10
Marmite	4
Salmon paste	17
Sardine and tomato paste (1 tbsp)	17
Tuna and mayonnaise paste	17

SUGAR PER PORTION (G)	TEASPOONS OF SUGAR PER PORTION	SUGAR PER 100G	ENERGY (KCAL) PER 100G	SATURATES PER 100G	SALT PER 100G
8.9	2.2	59.0	239	0.1	trace
8.4	2.1	56.0	229	0.1	trace
7.8	2.0	52.0	211	0.1	trace
7.8	2.0	52.0	211	0.1	trace
5.3	1.3	26.7	562	7.5	0.30
7.5	1.9	49.9	334	1.8	0.2
trace	0.0	0.2	207	5.7	0.83
1.1	0.3	5.6	628	10.2	trace
trace	0.0	0.3	170	2.6	1.08
6.0	1.5	49.0	330	0.0	0.25
1.6	0.4	16.3	164	0.7	1.50
2.1	0.5	20.8	219	1.0	2.00
trace	0.0	1.1	252	trace	9.80
trace	0.0	0.6	200	3.6	1.00
0.2	0.0	1.4	167	2.6	1.48
trace	0.0	0.5	215	1.3	0.80

	AN AVERAGE PORTION EQUALS (G):
Branded chocolate bars	
Boost	49
Bounty	57
Bounty Dark	57
Bournville	45
Chocolate Orange bar	40
Chomp	24
Creme Egg Twisted	45
Crunchie	40
Curly Wurly	26
Dairy Milk	45
Dairy Milk, caramel	45
Dairy Milk, fruit and nut	49
Dairy Milk, wholenut	49
Double Decker	54
Flake	32
Flyte	23
Freddo	18
Freddo, caramel	20
Fry's Turkish Delight	51
Fudge	25
Galaxy	42
Galaxy, bubbles block	50
Galaxy, caramel block	45
Galaxy, cookie crumble block	57
Galaxy, Counters bag	35
Galaxy, Honeycomb bar	40
Galaxy, Minstrels	42
Galaxy, Ripple	42
KitKat, 70% dark (2 fingers)	21
KitKat, 70% dark (4 fingers)	45
KitKat, cookies and cream (2 fingers)	21
KitKat, milk chocolate (2 fingers)	21
KitKat, milk chocolate (4 fingers)	45

SUGAR PER PORTION (G)	TEASPOONS OF SUGAR PER PORTION	SUGAR PER 100G	ENERGY (KCAL) PER 100G	SATURATES PER 100G	SALT PER 100G
24.3	6.1	49.5	515	21.5	0.33
27.2	6.8	47.8	488	21.4	0.26
25.5	6.4	44.7	492	22.3	0.25
26.0	6.5	57.7	505	16.6	0.01
23.5	5.9	59.5	525	17.5	0.38
11.1	2.8	47.3	465	11.1	0.45
27.9	7.0	61.9	465	12.9	0.15
24.7	6.2	61.7	470	12.3	0.70
12.4	3.1	47.8	450	9.9	0.58
25.0	6.3	56.0	530	18.5	0.23
24.0	6.0	53.5	480	14.0	0.40
26.8	6.7	54.7	500	15.2	0.20
24.5	6.1	49.9	545	16.8	0.20
30.0	7.5	55.5	465	12.0	0.20
17.7	4.4	55.2	530	19.1	0.28
15.4	3.9	68.3	432	7.7	2.25
10.2	2.6	56.7	530	18.5	0.23
10.3	2.6	52.7	490	14.9	0.35
29.5	7.4	57.7	365	4.1	0.30
16.3	4.1	64.0	440	8.6	0.35
23.3	5.8	55.4	544	19.4	0.28
27.7	6.9	54.1	555	20.4	0.28
25.0	6.3	55.6	483	14.4	0.40
30.3	7.6	53.2	550	20.5	0.25
20.6	5.1	58.8	529	17.0	0.28
22.9	5.7	57.2	547	20.0	0.25
28.9	7.2	68.9	503	13.0	0.20
19.3	4.8	58.5	527	16.9	0.28
8.9	2.2	42.2	505	16.0	0.08
12.0	3.0	26.4	535	21.6	0.04
10.6	2.7	50.7	510	15.4	0.20
10.4	2.6	49.5	512	15.9	0.13
22.8	5.7	50.1	513	15.9	0.14

CHOCOLATE

	AN AVERAGE PORTION EQUALS (G):
KitKat, mint (2 fingers)	21
KitKat, orange (2 fingers)	21
KitKat, chunky	48
KitKat, chunky peanut butter	48
M&M's, choco bag	45
M&M's, crispy bag	36
M&M's, peanut bag	45
Maltesers	37
Malteasers Teasers	35
Mars	51
Milky Way Magic Stars	33
Picnic	42
Revels	35
Snickers	48
Starbar	42
Timeout	42
Toffee Crisp	43
Topic	42
Twirl	42
Twix	42
Wispa	39
Wispa Gold	52
Yorkie	55

With sweets, it's all about how many you eat. Fact: you'll eat fewer sweets if you're forced to take your time, so go for those with wrappers.

Sweets

Chewitts (1 pack)	30
Dib Dab (1 pack)	23
Fruit sherbets (3 sweets)	24
Foam shrimps/banana	25
Fox's Glacier fruits (1 sweet)	5.5
Fox's Glacier mints (1 sweet)	5.5
Fudge, wrapped (3 sweets)	30
Haribo gold bears	25
Haribo, jelly sweets	25

SUGAR PER PORTION (G)	TEASPOONS OF SUGAR PER PORTION	SUGAR PER 100G	ENERGY (KCAL) PER 100G	SATURATES PER 100G	SALT PER 100G
10.4	2.6	49.5	512	15.9	0.13
10.4	2.6	49.5	512	15.9	0.13
23.7	5.9	49.3	515	16.3	0.15
22.7	5.7	47.3	541	16.3	0.10
29.9	7.5	66.4	479	12.5	0.23
19.4	4.9	53.9	496	15.9	0.43
24.1	6.0	53.6	506	10.1	0.15
19.7	4.9	53.2	505	15.1	0.38
18.7	4.7	53.3	532	17.8	0.33
30.4	7.6	59.7	449	8.3	0.41
17.6	4.4	53.3	555	21.2	0.20
22.9	5.7	47.4	475	10.6	0.65
22.3	5.6	63.6	480	12.6	0.30
21.7	5.4	45.2	510	9.6	0.45
20.5	5.1	41.8	505	15.2	0.30
14.8	3.7	45.4	530	10.6	0.20
21.2	5.3	48.2	520	18.3	0.22
25.6	6.4	54.4	494	7.7	0.43
23.4	5.8	55.6	535	19.1	0.25
20.5	5.1	48.8	495	13.9	0.44
20.5	5.1	52.5	550	21.0	0.23
23.8	6.0	45.8	510	17.3	0.40
31.1	7.8	56.6	546	18.6	0.16
14.7	3.7	49.0	385	2.0	0.25
18.7	4.7	81.4	386	0.3	2.19
17.4	4.4	72.7	410	1.2	trace
21.2	5.3	84.9	374	0.1	trace
4.0	1.0	70.8	265	trace	0.30
4.1	1.0	72.6	369	trace	trace
17.7	4.4	59.7	443	6.7	0.70
14.6	3.7	58.4	348	1.0	trace
14.6	3.7	58.4	348	trace	trace

CHOCOLATE AND SWEETS

	AN AVERAGE PORTION EQUALS (G):
Haribo, maom strips (3 strips)	21
Haribo sour cherries	25
Haribo starmix	25
Haribo strawbs	25
Haribo tangfastics	25
Jelly babies (8 sweets)	52
Jelly Belly beans (mini pouch)	40
Jelly Tots (12 sweets)	11
Liquorice Allsorts	48
Liquorice, traditional soft	40
M&S Percy Pigs (3 sweets)	26
Marshmallows (approx. 3 sweets)	21
Maynards wine gums (3 sweets)	18
Mint creams	25
Mint imperials (3 sweets)	8
Murray mints (approx. 4 sweets)	25
Polo (1 tube)	34
Polo, sugar free (1tube)	33
Randoms (7 sweets)	29
Refreshers (1 roll)	34
Rowntrees, fruit gums (8 sweets)	18
Rowntrees, fruit pastilles (1 tube)	53
Rowntrees, pick & mix (12 sweets)	33
Sherbet fountain	25
Toffee, wrapped (3 sweets)	24

Did you know? It's better to sweet treat all in one go rather than nibble over several hours – tooth decay is more related to the frequency of

SUGAR PER PORTION (G)	TEASPOONS OF SUGAR PER PORTION	SUGAR PER 100G	ENERGY (KCAL) PER 100G	SATURATES PER 100G	SALT PER 100G
12.5	3.1	59.5	394	3.2	0.03
14.6	3.7	58.4	348	*	trace
15.9	4.0	63.4	344	*	trace
14.6	3.7	58.4	348	*	trace
15.0	3.7	59.9	340	*	trace
39.6	9.9	75.4	335	trace	0.03
27.7	6.9	69.3	368	0.1	trace
6.9	1.7	60.9	351	0.0	0.50
29.5	7.4	62.2	380	3.5	0.10
14.8	3.7	37.1	323	1.0	0.25
19.2	0.0	74.0	335	trace	trace
13.0	3.3	62.0	329	trace	trace
10.2	2.6	57.3	325	0.2	0.05
23.0	5.7	91.8	365	0.0	trace
7.5	1.9	96.0	389	trace	0.45
13.7	3.4	54.0	055	2.2	0.28
32.5	8.1	95.7	402	1.0	trace
0.0	0.0	0.0	238	0.0	trace
17.2	4.3	59.1	328	0.3	0.10
30.2	7.6	88.7	380	0.7	2.76
8.0	2.0	43.8	328	trace	0.53
30.6	7.6	58.2	350	0.0	0.29
18.7	4.7	56.8	357	0.3	0.35
20.7	5.2	82.6	375	0.2	3.25
11.7	2.9	48.6	475	10.2	0.94

sugar hits you get than the total amount of sugar you eat overall.
* for an explanation of this symbol, see page 16.

CHOCOLATE
AND SWEETS

	AN AVERAGE PORTION EQUALS (G):
Crisps	
Bombay mix	50
Crisps, cheese and onion	25
Crisps, prawn cocktail	25
Crisps, ready salted	25
Crisps, salt and vinegar	25
Hula Hoops, bbq	24
Hula Hoops, original	24
Kettle Chips, lightly salted	50
Kettle Chips, mature cheddar	50
Kettle Chips, sea salt and cracked black pepper	50
Mini Cheddars	25
Mrs Crimbles original cheese bites	30
Popchips, barbecue	22
Popchips, original	11
Pretzels, salted	30
Pringles, original	30
Pringles, salt & vinegar	30
Pringles, sour cream & onion	30
Pringles, Texas bbq sauce	30
Quavers, cheese	16
Skips, prawn cocktail	16
Snack a Jacks, salt and vinegar	22
Snack a Jacks, sweet chilli	22
Special K cracker crisps, original sea salt	21
Special K cracker crisps, sea salt & balsamic vinegar	21
Special K cracker crisps, sweet chilli	21
Tyrell's, cheddar cheese and chive	50
Tyrell's, cider vinegar	50
Tyrrell's, habas fritas	40
Tyrell's, sweet chilli and red pepper	50

SUGAR PER PORTION (G)	TEASPOONS OF SUGAR PER PORTION	SUGAR PER 100G	ENERGY (KCAL) PER 100G	SATURATES PER 100G	SALT PER 100G
3.6	0.9	7.0	539	8.4	2.00
0.7	0.2	2.6	520	2.5	1.20
0.5	0.1	1.9	519	2.5	1.30
0.1	0.0	0.4	526	2.6	1.40
0.3	0.1	1.0	519	2.5	1.70
0.2	0.1	1.0	505	2.5	2.30
trace	0.0	trace	507	2.5	1.80
0.3	0.1	0.5	513	3.5	0.90
1.3	0.3	2.5	505	3.3	1.10
0.4	0.1	0.8	502	3.3	1.50
1.2	0.3	4.6	522	11.9	2.30
0.2	0.1	0.5	439	7.6	3.00
1.6	0.4	7.3	432	1.6	2.00
0.2	0.1	2.2	413	1.8	1.90
0.5	0.1	1.8	393	0.5	1.50
0.4	0.1	1.4	522	5.0	1.40
1.1	0.3	3.8	512	5.0	2.30
1.0	0.3	3.2	515	5.0	1.60
1.3	0.3	4.2	511	5.0	1.60
0.7	0.2	4.1	534	2.7	2.20
1.3	0.3	8.1	530	2.6	2.30
0.4	0.1	1.8	406	0.8	2.80
0.6	0.1	2.7	414	0.8	2.20
0.7	0.2	3.5	406	1.5	2.20
1.9	0.5	9.0	411	1.5	2.60
1.3	0.4	6.0	409	1.5	2.20
1.6	0.4	3.1	486	2.9	1.25
1.2	0.3	2.3	447	2.5	1.50
1.7	0.4	4.3	210	4.0	1.25
1.9	0.5	3.7	490	2.6	1.50

Popcorn kernels are a handy store cupboard staple that can be popped at home and act as a great blank canvas for many sugar-free flavour variations, such as a sprinkling of paprika or cinnamon.

AN AVERAGE
PORTION EQUALS
(G):

Tyrell's, Thai chilli crackers	50
Tyrell's, veg crisps	40
Walkers Baked, cheese and onion	25
Walkers Baked, ready salted	25
Walkers Baked, salt and vinegar	25
Walkers Lights, ready salted	24
Wotsits, cheese	19

Popcorn

Butterkist, salted	40
Butterkist, sweet cinema style	40
Butterkist, toffee	50
Heston from Waitrose salted caramel	25
Metcalfe's Skinny Topcorn, heat and sweet	25
Metcalfe's Skinny Topcorn, sweet and salty	25
Salted	25
Sweet and salty	25
Sweet	25
Toffee	50
Tyrell's, sticky toffee pudding	38
Tyrell's, sweet and salty	40

Dips

Beetroot and sesame dip	45
Cheddar cheese and chive dip	45
Doritos, hot salsa dip	40
Doritos, mild salsa dip	40
Doritos, nacho cheese dip	40
Doritos, sour cream & chive dip (2 tbsp)	40
Guacamole	43
Guacamole, Reduced Fat	43
Houmous	46

SUGAR PER PORTION (G)	TEASPOONS OF SUGAR PER PORTION	SUGAR PER 100G	ENERGY (KCAL) PER 100G	SATURATES PER 100G	SALT PER 100G
6.5	1.6	13.0	520	16.2	2.50
9.0	2.3	22.5	506	4.1	1.50
1.8	0.5	7.0	411	0.8	0.90
1.5	0.4	5.8	410	0.8	1.20
1.6	0.4	6.3	406	0.8	0.90
0.1	0.0	0.5	480	2.0	1.50
1.3	0.3	6.6	546	4.0	2.00
0.5	0.1	1.2	475	3.2	0.90
10.3	2.6	25.8	525	4.2	trace
33.1	8.3	66.1	420	1.9	1.40
14.6	3.7	58.4	433	3.3	1.50
5.0	1.2	19.9	446	1.4	1.37
4.9	1.2	19.6	459	1.5	1.35
0.1	0.0	0.5	535	2.3	1.90
3.1	0.8	12.3	536	4.2	0.88
7.7	1.9	30.9	515	2.6	trace
29.8	7.5	59.6	420	1.7	0.14
8.3	2.1	22.0	504	2.0	0.25
8.2	2.1	20.5	507	2.8	1.50
2.0	0.5	4.4	145	1.7	1.20
0.6	0.1	1.3	355	6.6	1.23
1.6	0.4	4.0	13	trace	0.56
1.6	0.4	4.1	33	0.1	1.38
1.3	0.3	3.3	231	3.3	1.03
1.3	0.3	3.2	244	3.8	0.98
1.2	0.3	2.9	212	7.4	0.50
0.5	0.1	1.1	146	2.9	0.50
0.3	0.1	0.7	278	2.7	0.63

CRISPS, DIPS AND NIBBLES

	AN AVERAGE PORTION EQUALS (G):
Houmous, caramelised onion	50
Houmous, moroccan topped	50
Houmous, piri piri	50
Houmous, red pepper, reduced fat	50
Houmous, reduced fat	46
Houmous, roasted red pepper	50
Houmous, smoky jalapeno topped	50
Houmous, tomato and basil, reduced fat	50
Moroccan butternut dip	45
Onion and garlic dip	46
Sabra, houmous extra (2 tbsp)	30
Sabra, houmous with garlic and red pepper (2 tbsp)	30
Salsa dip (2 tbsp)	**30**
Smoked salmon taramasalata	50
Soured cream and chive dip, reduced fat	46
Taramasalata, smoked salmon	46
Taramasalata, standard	46
Tzatziki	46

Antipasti

Artichoke antipasti	40
Capers	15
Chargrilled vegetables in herb dressing	**50**
Cheese and onion	50
Courgette antipasti	43
Falafels	50
Falafels, beetroot	**50**
Gherkins, drained (1 large)	39
Hot cherry peppers, ricotta stuffed	**50**
Mozzarella with semi-dried tomatoes	80
Olives with garlic and chilli dressing	50
Olives with sweet pepper and basil dressing	50

SUGAR PER PORTION (G)	TEASPOONS OF SUGAR PER PORTION	SUGAR PER 100G	ENERGY (KCAL) PER 100G	SATURATES PER 100G	SALT PER 100G
2.4	0.6	4.7	280	2.2	1.20
1.3	0.3	2.5	225	2.1	0.78
1.3	0.3	2.6	290	2.3	1.01
0.8	0.2	1.6	140	0.7	0.99
0.3	0.1	0.6	179	1.5	1.09
1.3	0.3	2.6	317	2.6	0.89
1.0	0.2	1.9	267	2.2	0.88
0.7	0.2	1.3	155	1.0	1.05
1.6	0.4	3.5	123	0.5	0.90
1.3	0.3	2.8	331	5.3	1.00
0.1	0.0	0.4	341	2.4	1.13
0.1	0.0	0.3	339	2.4	1.25
2.3	0.6	7.5	62	0.2	0.45
0.6	0.2	1.2	475	3.8	1.33
1.7	0.4	3.6	176	4.0	0.40
0.6	0.1	1.2	493	3.3	1.20
0.6	0.2	1.2	493	3.3	1.20
1.3	0.3	2.9	129	4.4	0.57
0.2	0.1	0.5	85	0.7	2.00
0.3	0.1	2.0	27	0.0	8.66
3.4	0.8	6.7	79	0.0	2.68
1.0	0.2	1.9	344	10.3	1.33
1.2	0.3	2.8	59	0.4	2.30
1.2	0.3	2.4	263	0.9	1.50
3.5	0.9	7.0	257	1.4	0.76
2.2	0.6	5.5	31	trace	1.30
6.1	1.5	12.1	181	4.1	0.78
3.8	1.0	4.8	194	4.9	0.80
trace	0.0	trace	119	1.1	3.60
trace	0.0	trace	166	2.0	2.70

CRISPS, DIPS
AND NIBBLES 61

	AN AVERAGE PORTION EQUALS (G):
Olive, pimento stuffed	15
Peppers, feta stuffed	36
Roasted pepper antipasti	42
Stuffed vine leaves (1 vine leaf)	31
Sun dried tomatoes in oil	70
Sunkiss/blush tomatoes in oil	60
Unearthed black peppper and rosemary olives	50
Unearthed olives and gouda	50

Deli fillers

Cheese and onion	50
Chicken, bacon and sweetcorn	50
Chicken tikka	50
Coronation chicken	50
Egg and bacon	50
Egg mayo	50
Princes Deli Fillers, tuna mediterranean	50
Princes Deli Fillers, tuna New York deli	50
Princes Deli Fillers, tuna Thai mayo	50
Seafood cocktail	50
Tuna and sweetcorn	50
Tuna crunch	50

* for an explanation of this symbol, see page 16.

SUGAR PER PORTION (G)	TEASPOONS OF SUGAR PER PORTION	SUGAR PER 100G	ENERGY (KCAL) PER 100G	SATURATES PER 100G	SALT PER 100G
trace	*	0.1	140	2.4	5.00
4.8	1.2	13.2	223	3.0	0.60
3.9	1.0	9.1	95	0.8	2.00
0.6	0.2	1.8	126	1.0	1.87
3.7	0.9	5.3	327	5.3	2.75
6.6	1.7	11.0	146	0.7	1.07
0.1	0.0	0.1	236	5.1	3.10
0.2	0.0	0.3	183	6.1	2.90
1.0	0.2	1.9	344	10.3	1.33
1.2	0.3	2.4	208	1.8	0.99
1.8	0.5	3.6	214	1.4	0.82
4.6	1.2	9.2	220	1.6	0.55
0.4	0.1	0.8	194	2.2	1.05
0.5	0.1	1.0	180	1.3	1.08
1.8	0.4	3.5	149	0.7	1.00
1.1	0.3	2.2	173	1.1	1.00
2.0	0.5	4.0	159	2.0	1.00
1.9	0.5	3.7	216	1.3	1.47
1.4	0.3	2.7	188	1.1	0.81
1.2	0.3	2.4	175	0.9	0.93

CRISPS, DIPS AND NIBBLES

Watch for flavoured and coated nuts, such as honey roasted or spicy varieties – it's often the case that they are quite high in both sugar and salt.

	AN AVERAGE PORTION EQUALS (G):
Nuts	
Almonds, blanched	25
Almonds, natural	25
Almonds, roasted and salted	25
Brazil nuts	25
Cashews, roasted and salted	25
Cashews, natural	25
Chestnuts, kernel only	25
Hazelnuts	25
KP Jumbo Cashews, honey roasted	25
KP Jumbo Peanuts, salt and vinegar	25
KP Jumbo Peanuts, spicy chilli	25
KP Peanuts, honey roasted	25
Macadamia nuts, salted	25
Mixed nuts, salted	25
Peanuts, bbq coated	50
Peanuts, chocolate	**50**
Peanuts, dry roasted	25
Peanuts, crunchy coated, chilli	50
Peanuts, plain	25
Peanuts, salted	25
Peanuts, sweet chilli coated	50
Pecans, plain	25
Pine nuts (1 tbsp)	12
Pistachios, roasted and salted, shelled	25
Tyrell's, spicy peanuts	25
Walnuts, plain	25
Wasabi peas	50
Seeds	
Flax (linseed) seed (1 tbsp)	11
Pumpkin seeds (1 tbsp)	11
Sunflower seeds (1 tbsp)	11

SUGAR PER PORTION (G)	TEASPOONS OF SUGAR PER PORTION	SUGAR PER 100G	ENERGY (KCAL) PER 100G	SATURATES PER 100G	SALT PER 100G
1.1	0.3	4.2	612	4.4	trace
1.0	0.2	3.9	592	3.7	trace
1.4	0.3	5.4	630	4.0	1.10
0.6	0.2	2.4	682	16.4	trace
1.4	0.4	5.6	611	10.1	0.89
1.5	0.4	5.9	595	7.8	trace
1.8	0.4	7.0	170	0.5	trace
1.0	0.3	4.0	650	4.7	trace
4.2	1.0	16.7	593	9.3	0.80
1.4	0.3	5.4	587	8.7	1.50
1.4	0.3	5.5	585	8.6	1.50
4.3	1.1	17.3	568	8.1	0.80
1.0	0.3	4.0	748	11.2	1.00
1.0	0.3	4.0	607	8.4	0.88
4.4	1.1	8.8	483	2.9	2.40
17.4	4.3	34.7	555	12.4	0.16
1.0	0.2	3.8	589	8.9	2.00
4.5	1.1	9.0	461	2.7	3.33
1.6	0.4	0.2	503	8.7	trace
1.0	0.2	3.8	602	9.5	1.30
2.7	0.7	5.3	530	8.2	2.90
1.1	0.3	4.3	689	5.7	trace
0.5	0.1	3.9	688	4.6	trace
1.4	0.4	5.7	601	7.4	1.65
4.5	1.1	17.9	486	4.8	1.50
0.7	0.2	2.6	688	5.6	trace
4.8	1.2	9.6	406	4.9	1.35
0.2	0.0	1.6	515	3.7	trace
0.2	0.0	1.4	593	8.7	0.10
0.2	0.0	1.7	581	4.5	trace

AN AVERAGE
PORTION EQUALS

Burger King

Big King	1 burger
Chicken Royale	1 burger
Double Rodeo	1 burger
French Fries	1 medium fries
Hamburger	**1 burger**
Ocean Catch Burger	1 burger
Onion Rings (regular)	8 rings
Steak House	1 burger
Vegebean Burger	1 burger
WHOPPER®	1 burger

Domino's Pizza (slices from a large pizza)

Americano Hot, dominator	1 slice
Domino's Deluxe, thin crust	1 slice
Extravaganza, dominator	1 slice
Farmhouse, classic crust	1 slice
Hawaiian, dominator	1 slice
Meat Lovers, thin crust	1 slice
New Yorker, classic crust	1 slice
Original Cheese and Tomato, thin crust	1 slice
Peperoni Passion®, stuffed crust	1 slice
Texas BBQ®, stuffed crust	**1 slice**
Vegi Volcano, classic crust	1 slice

KFC

BBQ Beans	1 regular beans
BBQ Rancher Twister®	1 Twister®
Corn Cobette	1 standard
Fries	1 regular fries
Kream Ball®, Caramel Fudge	**1 ball**
Original Recipe® Chicken on Bone	2 pieces
Original Recipe® Fillet Burger	1 burger
Original Recipe® Mini Breast Fillets	1 portion

For fast food chain drinks and milkshakes see pages 124–125.

SUGAR PER PORTION (G)	TEASPOONS OF SUGAR PER PORTION	SUGAR PER 100G	ENERGY (KCAL) PER 100G	SATURATES PER 100G	SALT PER 100G
6.6	1.7	3.6	256	5.1	1.08
6.6	1.7	3.1	288	2.0	1.71
8.4	2.1	4.6	273	5.6	0.93
0.2	0.1	0.2	247	3.4	1.27
6.0	1.5	5.3	240	3.2	1.22
4.4	1.1	2.2	255	2.8	1.30
4.3	1.1	3.6	297	3.8	0.30
12.8	3.2	4.8	273	6.0	1.12
12.7	3.2	4.5	223	3.1	1.25
11.8	3.0	4.0	224	3.4	0.89
4.4	1.1	3.0	312	6.2	1.20
1.9	3.0	3.0	312	6.2	1.20
3.8	1.0	3.0	266	4.6	1.00
3.4	0.9	3.9	222	3.1	1.00
4.3	1.1	3.8	252	3.3	1.00
1.7	0.4	2.4	318	6.7	1.50
3.1	0.8	3.1	258	3.3	1.50
2.7	0.7	5.0	239	3.5	1.20
3.5	0.9	3.5	283	7.1	1.60
8.8	2.2	9.1	266	5.4	1.30
3.8	1.0	4.2	222	3.6	0.80
7.7	1.9	6.4	88	0.1	0.75
13.1	3.3	5.5	194	1.8	0.92
1.9	0.5	2.6	116	0.3	0.01
0.4	0.1	0.4	280	1.9	0.08
44.4	11.1	26.7	210	5.2	0.31
14.0	3.5	0.3	258	2.9	1.08
5.8	1.5	2.9	219	1.2	1.14
0.3	0.1	0.4	203	1.1	1.75

AN AVERAGE
PORTION EQUALS

Original Recipe® Zinger Burger	1 burger
Popcorn® Chicken	1 regular
Streetwise Sundae®, Strawberry	1 sundae

McDonalds

Apple Pie	1 pie
Big Mac	1 burger
Chicken McNuggets	6 nuggets
Chocolate Muffin	**1 muffin**
Crispy Chicken and Bacon Salad	1 salad
Filet-O-Fish	1 burger
Fries	1 medium fries
Low Fat Balsamic Dressing	1 pot
Low Fat Caesar Dressing	1 pot
McChicken Sandwich	1 sandwich
Quarter Pounder with Cheese	1 burger
Smokey BBQ Dip	**1 pot**
Sour Cream and Chive Dip	1 pot
Strawberry Sundae	1 sundae
Sweet Chilli Dip	1 pot

SUGAR PER PORTION (G)	TEASPOONS OF SUGAR PER PORTION	SUGAR PER 100G	ENERGY (KCAL) PER 100G	SATURATES PER 100G	SALT PER 100G
5.7	1.4	2.9	231	1.4	1.23
0.6	0.2	0.6	279	2.6	1.58
23.0	5.8	21.9	176	3.36	0.26
10.0	2.5	11.9	297	3.3	0.55
8.0	2.0	3.9	239	4.9	1.02
0.5	0.1	0.5	240	1.7	0.6
36.0	9.0	29.0	415	4.0	0.73
5.0	1.3	1.8	137	1.1	0.47
6.0	1.5	4.1	229	2.1	0.89
1.0	0.3	0.6	198	1.2	0.36
4.0	1.0	12.1	76	0.0	2.73
3.0	0.8	4.8	64	1.6	1.43
7.0	1.8	4.1	226	1.2	0.94
10.0	2.5	5.4	265	7.0	1.19
15.0	3.8	30.0	170	0.0	1.80
0.0	0.0	0.0	320	4.0	1.20
45.0	11.3	24.8	160	2.8	0.11
25.0	6.3	50.0	240	0.0	1.60

AN AVERAGE
PORTION EQUALS
(G):

Supermarket and branded meals

Battered sweet and sour chicken	200
Beef in black bean sauce and rice	450
Chicken balti with pilau rice	500
Chicken choi mein	450
Chicken jalfrezi and pilau rice	500
Chicken korma with rice	500
Chicken tikka masala with rice	500
Chilli con carne and rice	450
Cottage pie	450
Crispy beef with sweet chilli sauce	**250**
Fish pie	450
Ham and mushroom tagliatelle	400
Lasagne	400
Linda McCartney lentil cottage pie	400
M&S Count on Us, chicken and asparagus risotto	385
M&S Count on Us, chicken in a creamy mushroom sauce, new potatoes and green beans	370
M&S Count on Us, fish pie	400
M&S Count on Us, king prawn masala with spiced pilau rice	370
M&S Count on Us, wok fried beef, chilli and ginger noodles	370
M&S Fuller Longer, chicken and vegetable casserole with sage and onion dumplings	440
M&S Fuller Longer, cod rogan balti	385
M&S Fuller Longer, paella with chicken and king prawns	390
Macaroni cheese	400
Mushroom risotto	400
Paella	400

SUGAR PER PORTION (G)	TEASPOONS OF SUGAR PER PORTION	SUGAR PER 100G	ENERGY (KCAL) PER 100G	SATURATES PER 100G	SALT PER 100G
31.6	7.9	15.8	169	0.3	0.58
7.2	1.8	1.6	130	0.6	0.68
9.5	2.4	1.9	153	0.5	0.57
7.2	1.8	1.6	124	0.4	0.78
9.5	2.4	1.9	156	0.5	0.56
7.0	1.8	1.4	158	2.5	0.49
22.0	5.5	4.4	178	2.3	0.60
8.6	2.1	1.9	126	1.0	0.40
3.2	0.8	0.7	93	1.8	0.55
47.3	11.8	18.9	108	1.3	0.56
3.2	0.8	0.7	95	1.8	0.30
4.8	1.2	1.2	137	2.6	0.57
9.6	2.4	2.4	157	4.0	0.55
10.8	2.7	2.7	94	1.0	0.40
4.6	1.2	1.2	94	0.8	0.40
3.3	0.8	0.9	76	0.7	0.33
2.0	0.5	0.5	83	1.1	0.45
5.9	1.5	1.6	88	0.1	0.35
4.8	1.2	1.3	87	0.5	0.48
5.7	1.4	1.3	105	1.3	0.53
6.9	1.7	1.8	90	0.9	0.50
2.7	0.7	0.7	110	0.7	0.40
4.4	1.1	1.1	194	4.9	0.55
3.6	0.9	0.9	130	2.9	0.60
4.0	1.0	1.0	132	1.0	0.60

Sugar levels are rarely a big concern in savoury main meals. Exceptions are sweet and sour and sweet chilli dishes.

PREPARED MEALS AND SANDWICHES

	AN AVERAGE PORTION EQUALS (G):
Quorn, chicken style and mushroom pie	235
Quorn, chilli and wedges	400
Quorn, classic lasagne	500
Quorn, cottage pie	500
Quorn, stew and dumplings	400
Quorn, tikka masala & rice	400
Reduced fat chilli con carne and rice	400
Singapore noodles	450
Spaghetti and meatballs	400
Spaghetti bolognese	400
Spaghetti carbonara	400
Spinach and ricotta cannelloni	400
Sweet and sour chicken with rice	**450**
Thai Green curry and rice	450
Thai red curry and rice	450
Weight Watchers, bolognese Al forno	380
Weight Watchers, chicken tikka	380
Weight Watchers, cottage pie	400
Weight Watchers, red Thai chicken curry	400
Weight Watchers, sausages in gravy	400

Breaded and battered foods

Battered onion rings	50
Breaded chicken goujons	61
Breaded chicken goujons, southern fried	61
Breaded chicken Kiev, garlic (1 kiev)	130
Breaded chicken Kiev, ham & cheese Filled (1 kiev)	130
Breaded cod fillet	150
Chicken dippers (4 dippers)	70
Fish fingers (3 fingers)	75
Salmon fish cakes	150

SUGAR PER PORTION (G)	TEASPOONS OF SUGAR PER PORTION	SUGAR PER 100G	ENERGY (KCAL) PER 100G	SATURATES PER 100G	SALT PER 100G
3.3	0.8	1.4	219	5.1	0.80
12.0	3.0	3.0	78	0.3	0.48
8.0	2.0	1.6	99	1.6	0.45
8.0	2.0	1.6	73	1.0	0.40
8.0	2.0	2.0	108	1.9	0.80
8.8	2.2	2.2	103	1.8	0.80
10.0	2.5	2.5	105	1.1	0.51
6.8	1.7	1.5	159	0.7	0.63
12.4	3.1	3.1	118	1.6	0.46
9.6	2.4	2.4	162	2.8	0.51
4.4	1.1	1.1	156	3.7	0.70
12.4	3.1	3.1	155	5.0	0.49
53.1	13.3	11.8	159	0.3	0.38
5.0	1.2	1.1	151	3.8	0.58
9.5	2.4	2.1	148	3.3	0.54
9.5	2.4	2.5	90	1.1	0.40
5.3	1.3	1.4	90	0.3	0.40
5.2	1.3	1.3	87	1.2	0.40
4.4	1.1	1.1	95	1.8	0.50
9.6	2.4	2.4	85	0.9	0.50
1.9	0.5	3.8	116	0.7	0.6
0.8	0.2	1.3	255	1.2	0.87
0.9	0.2	1.4	258	0.7	0.58
1.0	0.3	0.8	283	0.8	1.05
0.8	0.2	0.6	236	3.0	1.00
2.1	0.5	1.4	194	0.6	1.0
0.4	0.1	0.6	249	1.7	1.0
0.2	0.1	0.3	202	1.0	0.9
6.3	1.6	4.2	221	1.5	0.6

AN AVERAGE
PORTION EQUALS
(G):

Scampi	150
Young's battered calamari	125

Pies, pasties and quiches

Ginsters, chicken & mushroom slice	170
Ginsters, cornish pasty	130
Ginsters, cornish pasty, large	284
Ginsters, peppered steak slice	170
Ginsters, ploughmans roll	130
Ginsters, sausage roll	60
Ginsters, sausage roll, large	130
Ginsters, spicy chicken slice	170
Ginsters, steak slice	105
Higgidy, balsamic onion & cheddar quiche (⅓ of the quiche)	133
Higgidy, little cheddar & ham quiche	155
Higgidy, little mushroom & tomato quiche	155
Higgidy, little spinach & feta quiche	155
Higgidy, spinach, feta & roasted pepper quiche (⅓ of the quiche)	133
Pukka Pies, all steak pie	233
Pukka Pies, chicken & mushroom pie	226
Weight Watchers, crustless bacon & leek quiche	160
Weight Watchers, crustless cheese & onion quiche	160

Supermarket and branded sandwiches

BLT	1 pack
Cheddar and chutney, deep fill	1 pack
Cheese and onion	1 pack
Chicken and bacon	1 pack
Chicken salad	1 pack
Corned beef and pickle	1 pack

SUGAR PER PORTION (G)	TEASPOONS OF SUGAR PER PORTION	SUGAR PER 100G	ENERGY (KCAL) PER 100G	SATURATES PER 100G	SALT PER 100G
2.0	0.5	1.3	203	0.6	0.6
0.3	0.1	0.3	208	1.3	1.20
2.0	0.5	1.2	290	9.9	0.89
2.3	0.6	1.8	249	7.2	1.17
5.1	1.3	1.8	249	7.2	1.17
2.0	0.5	1.2	307	9.9	0.86
3.9	1.0	3	346	11.2	1.17
0.7	0.2	1.2	327	9.4	1.08
0.9	0.2	0.7	393	12.7	1.41
3.2	0.8	1.9	308	9.2	0.72
1.1	0.3	1	295	9.2	0.94
4.7	1.2	3.5	290	8.5	0.6
2.6	0.7	1.7	265	7.1	0.6
3.6	0.9	2.3	271	7.6	0.6
2.9	0.7	1.9	257	7.6	0.7
2.7	0.7	2	295	7.1	0.43
2.6	0.6	1.1	229	5.4	1
0.7	0.2	0.3	210	5	1
3.5	0.9	2.2	188	4.3	0.5
2.7	0.7	1.7	167	4	0.9
3.7	0.9	2.3	218	2.0	1.22
19.3	**4.8**	**7.8**	**242**	**5.9**	**0.86**
2.7	0.7	1.7	272	6.7	0.78
3.5	0.9	2.3	218	2.0	1.33
7.3	1.8	3.6	171	0.5	0.85
7.2	1.8	4.7	239	3.9	1.46

	AN AVERAGE PORTION EQUALS (G):
Egg mayo	1 pack
M&S, Count on Us, British chicken with a mayo free dressing on soft wholemeal	151
M&S, Count on Us, British smoked ham salad and mustard dressing	218
M&S, Count on Us, chargrilled chicken with a basil dressing and roasted tomatoes	171
M&S, Count on Us, smoked turkey and pastrami	224
M&S, Count on Us, Tuna, cucumber and salad cream dressing on oatmeal bread	202
M&S, Fuller Longer, smokey chilli beef and cheese wrap	210
Prawn mayo	1 pack
Pret A Manger, hoisin duck salad wrap	1 pack
Pret A Manger, Pole and line caught tuna mayo and cucumber baguette	1 baguette
Pret A Manger, Wild crayfish and rocket	1 pack
Pret A Manger, Wiltshire cured ham and pickle	1 pack
Salmon and cucumber	1 pack
Subway, beef low fat 6 inch sub	219
Subway, chicken temptation 6 inch sub	262
Subway, meatball marinara 6 inch sub	300
Subway, eteak & cheese 6 inch sub	245
Subway, club low fat 6 inch sub	252
Subway, tuna 6 inch sub	233
Subway, veggie delite low fat 6 inch sub	162
Subway, veggie patty 6 inch sub	247

SUGAR PER PORTION (G)	TEASPOONS OF SUGAR PER PORTION	SUGAR PER 100G	ENERGY (KCAL) PER 100G	SATURATES PER 100G	SALT PER 100G
2.7	0.7	1.6	217	1.2	0.70
1.4	0.3	0.9	173	0.9	0.73
3.9	1.0	1.8	127	0.4	0.78
2.6	0.6	1.5	169	0.7	0.85
3.4	0.8	1.5	126	0.7	0.65
5.1	1.3	2.5	141	0.3	0.83
1.5	0.4	0.7	165	2.2	0.73
2.4	0.6	1.4	230	0.9	1.00
12.8	3.2	5.8	170	1.4	1.02
8.0	2.0	3.5	211	0.6	1.09
2.7	0.7	1.4	191	0.9	0.90
12.2	3.1	5.1	153	0.7	1.04
3.5	0.9	1.9	180	0.9	0.74
5.1	1.3	2.3	129	0.6	0.5
5.3	1.3	2.0	155	1.3	0.7
10.9	2.7	3.6	145	2.2	0.6
6.4	1.6	2.6	140	1.8	0.7
5.4	1.3	2.1	123	0.6	0.7
5.0	1.3	2.2	152	0.6	0.7
4.8	1.2	3.0	131	0.4	0.4
7.9	2.0	3.2	154	1.1	0.7

PREPARED
MEALS AND
SANDWICHES **77**

Salads and sushi

Boots Delicious pesto pasta layered salad	200
Boots Delicious simply spicy chicken pasta salad	300
Boots Shapers chilli chicken layered pasta salad	174
Boots Shapers hoisin duck sushi	121
Boots Shapers smoked salmon sushi	118
Boots Shapers tuna nicoise layered pasta salad	200
Boots Shapers veggie sushi	115
M&S barbecue pulled pork pasta salad	320
M&S beetroot, goat's cheese and lentil salad	290
M&S fish sushi selection	174
M&S sweet chilli chicken noodle salad	295
Pret A Manger chefs Italian chicken salad (with dressing)	337
Pret A Manger crayfish and quinoa protein pot	168
Pret A Manger deluxe sushi	232
Pret A Manger salmon, prawn and crab sushi	230
Pret A Manger superfood salad (with dressing)	443
Pret A Manger veggie sushi	226
Pret A Manger Vietnamese pullled pork salad	296

SUGAR PER PORTION (G)	TEASPOONS OF SUGAR PER PORTION	SUGAR PER 100G	ENERGY (KCAL) PER 100G	SATURATES PER 100G	SALT PER 100G
4.7	1.2	2.4	106	0.7	0.39
12.0	3.0	4.1	159	0.4	0.34
10.0	2.5	5.8	75	trace	0.48
15.0	3.8	12.0	146	0.5	0.68
13.0	3.3	11.0	154	0.3	0.96
3.7	0.9	1.8	83	0.2	0.42
14.0	3.5	12.0	144	0.3	0.66
17.3	4.3	5.4	158	0.7	0.73
10.4	2.6	3.6	113	1.1	0.73
8.6	2.2	5.1	146	0.3	1.13
14.8	3.7	5.0	110	0.2	0.23
5.3	1.3	1.6	162	1.5	0.73
1.5	0.9	0.9	125	1.0	0.45
9.0	2.3	3.9	165	0.7	1.19
10.8	2.7	4.7	156	0.5	1.17
7.9	2.0	1.8	149	0.9	0.35
10.4	2.6	4.7	147	0.4	1.21
17.7	4.4	6.0	113	1.7	0.59

PREPARED
MEALS AND
SANDWICHES 79

AN AVERAGE
PORTION EQUALS
(G):

Soups

Baxter's lobster bisque	200
Campbell's, condensed cream of chicken	310
Campbell's, condensed cream of tomato	310
Carrot and coriander, fresh	300
Cream of mushroom, canned	200
Cup a Soup, cream of mushroom (made up as directed)	1 sachet
Cup a Soup Special, minestrone with croutons (made up as directed)	1 sachet
Cup a Soup, tomato (made up as directed)	1 sachet
Cup a Soup Special, tomato and veg with croutons (made up as directed)	1 sachet
Glorious, Tolouse Sausage and Bean Cassoulet	300
Glorious, Tuscan Chicken and Orzo	300
Glorious, West African Chicken and Peanut	300
Heinz, cream of chicken	200
Heinz, cream of tomato	200
Heinz Big Soup, beef and veg	200
Heinz Big Soup, chicken and veg	200
Heinz Big Soup, minted lamb hotpot	200
Itsu miso soup (made up to 200g with water)	1 sachet
New Covent Garden, lentil and smoked bacon	300
New Covent Garden, maris piper potato and leek	300
New Covent Garden, pea, ham and leek	300
New Covent Garden, wild mushroom	300
Tomato and basil, fresh	300

Soups have received a bad press, but most get green lights for sugar. You could just avoid the tomato ones if you're concerned – they tend to be higher in natural sugars than the others.

SUGAR PER PORTION (G)	TEASPOONS OF SUGAR PER PORTION	SUGAR PER 100G	ENERGY (KCAL) PER 100G	SATURATES PER 100G	SALT PER 100G
4.4	1.1	2.2	68	2.7	0.60
1.2	0.3	0.4	48	0.4	0.58
22.3	5.6	7.2	79	0.4	0.58
9.6	2.4	3.2	36	0.9	0.50
1.8	0.5	0.9	54	0.6	0.60
2.6	0.7	1.0	47	1.4	0.58
4.8	1.2	1.9	36	0.3	0.50
8.8	2.2	3.5	35	0.4	0.50
7.4	1.9	2.8	43	0.5	0.50
9.3	2.3	3.1	64	0.6	0.50
9.0	2.3	3.0	40	trace	0.60
6.6	1.7	2.2	95	2.8	0.50
2.4	0.6	1.2	51	0.5	0.60
10.0	2.5	5.0	59	0.2	0.60
3.8	1.0	1.9	53	0.4	0.60
3.6	0.9	1.8	50	0.2	0.50
5.0	1.3	2.5	58	0.5	0.60
3.7	0.9	1.9	21	trace	1.20
4.2	1.1	1.4	67	0.3	0.70
5.4	1.4	1.8	36	0.9	0.50
6.9	1.7	2.3	52	0.5	0.60
2.7	0.7	0.9	27	0.8	0.60
16.5	4.1	5.5	38	0.2	0.43

SOUPS AND NOODLES

AN AVERAGE
PORTION EQUALS
(G):

Veg and noodle pots

Innocent, Indian daal veg pot	380
Innocent, Japanese ramen noodle pot	380
Innocent, Mexican veg pot	390
Innocent, Thai curry veg pot	390
Innocent, Thai tom yum noodle pot	380
Innocent, Vietnamese curry noodle pot	380

Pot noodles (the add-water type)

Batchelors Cup-a-Noodle, curry (1 pot, prepared weight)	248
Batchelors Noodle Pot Shot, sweet & sour (1 pot, prepared weight)	248
Pot Noodle, chilli beef (1 pot, prepared weight)	305
Pot Noodle, Jamaican jerk (1 pot, prepared weight)	305
Pot Noodle, original curry (1 pot, prepared weight)	305
Pot Noodle, piri piri (1 pot, prepared weight)	305
Pot Noodle, snack chicken & mushroom (1 pot, prepared weight)	320
Pot Noodle, sticky rib (1 pot, prepared weight)	305

SUGAR PER PORTION (G)	TEASPOONS OF SUGAR PER PORTION	SUGAR PER 100G	ENERGY (KCAL) PER 100G	SATURATES PER 100G	SALT PER 100G
6.5	1.6	1.7	84	0.3	0.48
10.3	2.6	2.7	53	0.2	0.70
8.2	2.0	2.1	83	0.2	0.43
12.5	3.1	3.2	81	1.4	0.58
10.6	2.7	2.8	66	0.2	0.68
5.3	1.3	1.4	83	1.3	0.63
3.2	0.8	1.3	73	0.3	0.37
10.9	2.7	4.4	67	0.0	0.38
3.1	0.8	1.0	126	2.3	0.58
9.2	2.3	3.0	140	2.5	0.60
6.1	1.5	2.0	128	2.2	0.47
10.7	2.7	3.5	140	2.5	0.35
4.8	1.2	1.5	131	2.2	0.34
8.2	2.1	2.7	126	2.1	0.64

**AN AVERAGE
PORTION EQUALS
(G):**

Canned fish

John West Light Lunch, French tuna salad	220
John West Light Lunch, Mediterranean-style tuna salad	220
John West Tuna Steam Pot, chili garlic	285
John West Tuna Steam Pot, lemon thyme	285
John West Tuna Steam Pot, soy ginger	285
John West Tuna with a Twist, lime & pepper	85
John West Tuna with a Twist, tomato & herb dressing	85
John West Weight Watchers, tuna in tomato & herb dressing (1 tin)	80
John West Weight Watchers, tuna mayonnaise & sweetcorn (1 tin)	80
Mackerel fillets in olive oil (1 tin drained)	90
Mackerel fillets in tomato sauce (1 tin)	125
Mackerel pate	50
Prince's mackerel fillets in chilli sauce (1 tin)	125
Salmon, red (½ tin)	107
Sardines in brine (1 tin drained)	90
Sardines in olive oil (1 tin drained)	90
Sardines in tomato sauce (1 tin)	120
Tuna in sunflower oil (½ tin drained)	69
Tuna steaks in brine (1 small tin drained)	56
Tuna steaks in water (½ tin drained)	75

Processed meat

Corned beef (½ tin)	100
Ham, honey roast (3 wafer thin slices)	33
Ham, prosciutto (2 slices)	34
Pate, Ardennes, Brussels	30
Pate, duck and orange	30
Sausages premium, pork (1 sausage)	47
Sausages, pork, sweet chilli (1 sausage)	52

SUGAR PER PORTION (G)	TEASPOONS OF SUGAR PER PORTION	SUGAR PER 100G	ENERGY (KCAL) PER 100G	SATURATES PER 100G	SALT PER 100G
5.1	1.3	2.3	99	0.7	0.80
9.5	2.4	4.3	96	0.3	0.80
2.3	0.6	0.8	142	0.5	1.00
3.4	0.9	1.2	149	0.6	0.30
5.7	1.4	2.0	145	0.5	0.50
1.8	0.4	2.1	166	1.2	1.00
1.7	0.4	2.0	160	1.0	1.00
3.3	0.8	4.1	99	0.3	1.00
2.4	0.6	3.0	96	0.6	0.50
trace	0.0	trace	297	4.5	0.63
3.8	0.9	3.0	155	2.1	0.65
1.2	0.3	2.3	332	9.2	1.36
7.3	1.8	5.8	188	1.5	0.75
0.0	0.0	0.0	166	1.5	1.00
trace	0.0	trace	182	3.4	0.30
trace	0.0	trace	234	4.9	0.40
1.4	0.4	1.2	196	4.2	0.90
trace	0.0	trace	189	1.5	1.00
trace	0.0	trace	113	0.1	1.00
trace	0.0	trace	113	0.1	0.75
1.0	0.3	1.0	217	6.0	2.30
0.5	0.1	1.4	120	1.0	1.63
trace	0.0	trace	259	5.5	4.58
0.4	0.1	1.4	279	8.9	2.28
1.1	0.3	3.6	395	12.9	2.28
0.2	0.1	0.5	294	8.1	1.43
2.0	0.5	3.9	242	5.6	1.23

Eggs, fresh meat and fish don't contain any sugar, so we haven't listed these at all.

CANNED/
PROCESSED
FISH AND MEAT

AN AVERAGE
PORTION EQUALS

For a lower sugar biscuit choice, opt for an oat cake or rich tea.

Biscuits

Bourbon cream	1 biscuit
Cadbury's, Bournville biscuit	1 biscuit
Cadbury's, caramel biscuit	1 biscuit
Cadbury's, fingers	4 fingers
Choc chip cookie	1 biscuit
Chocolate coated ginger cookies, luxury, large	1 biscuit
Chocolate digestive, 30% less fat	1 biscuit
Club biscuit	1 biscuit
Coconut ring	1 biscuit
Cookie, soft bake, chocolate, giant	1 cookie
Cookie, soft bake, white chocolate and raspberry, giant	1 cookie
Custard cream,	1 biscuit
Digestive	1 biscuit
Fig roll	1 biscuit
Fox's Crunch cream	1 biscuit
Fruit shortcake	1 biscuit
Garibaldi	1 biscuit
Ginger nut	1 biscuit
Jaffa cake	1 biscuit
Jam sandwich cream	1 biscuit
Malted milk	1 biscuit
Maryland Gooeys, hazelnut	2 biscuits
Maryland Gooeys, triple chocolate	2 biscuits
Milk chocolate digestive	1 biscuit
Milk chocolate rich tea	1 biscuit
Morning coffee	1 biscuit
Nairns, dark choc chip oat biscuits	1 biscuit
Nairns, stem ginger oat biscuits	1 biscuit
Nice	1 biscuit
Pink wafers	1 biscuit
Plain chocolate digestive	1 biscuit

SUGAR PER PORTION (G)	TEASPOONS OF SUGAR PER PORTION	SUGAR PER 100G	ENERGY (KCAL) PER 100G	SATURATES PER 100G	SALT PER 100G
4.3	1.1	30.7	487	13.1	0.25
6.1	1.5	37.3	520	18.0	0.45
6.6	1.7	40.3	475	11.7	0.40
7.1	1.8	33.9	520	15.2	0.45
3.3	0.8	30.1	504	12.9	0.45
9.6	2.4	38.3	516	17.0	0.73
4.9	1.2	28.6	455	8.3	0.93
8.7	2.2	38.3	512	16.0	0.80
2.2	0.6	26.1	487	11.1	0.83
21.6	5.4	36.0	524	9.0	0.57
20.0	5.0	33.3	499	13.0	0.65
3.6	0.9	28.5	493	10.8	0.50
3.0	0.8	18.8	467	8.8	1.02
5.0	1.3	30.3	360	4.0	0.38
6.2	1.6	40.3	506	14.1	0.85
2.0	0.5	25.6	465	8.1	1.00
3.9	1.0	37.9	382	4.3	0.30
3.4	0.9	33.5	450	6.9	0.99
6.5	1.6	55.3	381	5.1	0.17
4.8	1.2	31.1	488	12.9	0.53
1.7	0.4	19.1	493	10.0	0.96
12.5	3.1	39.1	495	10.9	0.59
12.5	3.1	39.1	495	10.9	0.60
5.0	1.3	29.7	499	12.3	1.09
4.0	1.0	31.6	482	10.1	0.55
0.9	0.2	19.1	455	6.8	0.94
2.2	0.6	21.7	436	7.5	0.73
2.0	0.5	20.0	428	5.7	0.77
2.0	0.5	25.0	497	13.4	0.30
2.1	0.5	26.3	546	21.9	0.38
4.7	1.2	28.0	498	12.4	0.99

BISCUITS, SWEET AND SAVOURY

AN AVERAGE PORTION EQUALS

Rich tea	1 biscuit
Shortbread finger	1 biscuit
Shortcake	1 biscuit

Crackers and crispbreads

Butter puffs	1 puff
Cheese straws (1 straw)	10g
Cream crackers	1 cracker
Dietary Specials, light crispbread	1 slice
Dr Karg, emmental cheese and pumpkin (pack of mini crispbreads)	30g
Dr Karg, organic, sesame and linseed	30g
Finn crisp, original	1 slice
Itsu seaweed thins	5g
Jacob's crispbread, mixed seed	1 slice
Nairns cheese oatcakes	1 oatcake
Oatcakes	1 oatcake
Poppy and sesame thins	1 cracker
Ritz (7 crackers)	25g
Ryvita, crackerbread, original	1 slice
Ryvita, dark rye	1 slice
Ryvita, original	1 slice
Ryvita, pumpkin and oat	1 slice
Tuc	1 cracker
Tuc Sandwich	1 sandwich
Water biscuits	1 cracker

SUGAR PER PORTION (G)	TEASPOONS OF SUGAR PER PORTION	SUGAR PER 100G	ENERGY (KCAL) PER 100G	SATURATES PER 100G	SALT PER 100G
1.6	0.4	20.9	446	6.2	1.03
3.7	0.9	18.7	521	18.8	0.78
2.0	0.5	17.9	510	11.3	0.60
0.1	0.0	1.2	488	11.9	0.94
0.3	0.1	3.5	497	15.3	2.36
0.1	0.0	1.4	436	6.1	1.25
0.4	0.1	0.6	380	0.0	0.10
1.1	0.3	3.6	450	1.5	0.60
1.0	0.3	3.2	451	2.8	1.90
0.1	0.0	0.9	360	0.5	1.50
trace	0.0	trace	480	4.0	6.00
0.6	0.2	5.8	447	6.2	1.30
trace	0.0	0.6	473	12.0	2.80
0.3	0.1	2.7	445	5.0	1.40
0.1	0.0	2.1	488	9.4	1.84
2.1	0.5	8.6	500	10.5	1.38
0.1	0.0	0.5	378	0.4	1.05
0.3	0.1	3.0	342	0.2	0.74
0.3	0.1	2.9	350	0.3	0.50
0.6	0.2	4.9	370	1.3	0.61
0.3	0.1	7.0	518	13.5	2.50
0.5	0.1	4.0	531	15.6	1.50
0.1	0.0	1.8	412	3.0	1.12

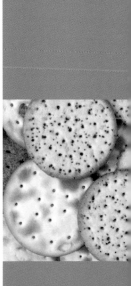

BISCUITS,
SWEET AND
SAVOURY

AN AVERAGE
PORTION EQUALS
(G):

Cakes and scones

Banana loaf (1 slice)	85
Battenberg (1 slice)	32
Cadbury's mini roll	27
Cake mix, made up (1 slice)	85
Chelsea bun (1 bun)	84
Chocolate cake, with fudge icing (1 slice)	98
Chocolate crispie cakes (1 cake)	25
Chocolate éclair, cream (1 small éclair)	35
Christmas cake (1 slice)	70
Coffee and walnut cake (1 slice)	69
Cream horn (1 small horn)	50
Cup cake, iced	65
Doughnut, jam	70
Eccles cake	66
Fruit cake (1 slice)	90
Fruit cake, rich (1 slice)	70
Gateau, chocolate, frozen (1 slice)	85
Gateau, fruit, frozen (1 slice)	85
Haribo iced cupcake	40
Iced fairy cake (1 cake)	40
Jam tart (1 tart)	39
Lemon drizzle cake, iced	72
Madeira (1 slice)	70
Millionaire's shortbread (1 slice)	38
Mr Kipling, almond slice	1 cake
Mr Kipling, angel slice	1 cake
Mr Kipling, apple & blackcurrant pie	1 pie
Mr Kipling, bakewell slice	1 cake
Mr Kipling, banoffee cake slice	1 cake
Mr Kipling, bramley apple pie	1 pie
Mr Kipling, cherry bakewell	1 pie
Mr Kipling, chocolate slice	1 cake
Mr Kipling, country slice	1 cake

SUGAR PER PORTION (G)	TEASPOONS OF SUGAR PER PORTION	SUGAR PER 100G	ENERGY (KCAL) PER 100G	SATURATES PER 100G	SALT PER 100G
30.9	7.7	36.3	388	2.4	0.40
11.8	2.9	36.8	373	3.4	1.08
11.4	2.8	42.2	450	11.3	0.68
24.1	6.0	28.3	322	6.0	0.07
13.8	3.4	16.4	291	2.2	0.45
43.5	10.9	44.4	358	4.6	0.66
10.7	2.7	42.8	461	10.7	0.77
6.0	1.5	17.1	393	12.6	0.30
40.8	10.2	58.3	350	1.8	0.29
27.5	6.9	39.8	460	7.7	0.40
9.1	2.3	18.1	410	13.3	0.55
34.2	8.5	52.6	500	10.7	0.30
13.2	3.3	18.8	336	4.3	0.45
14.6	3.6	22.1	387	8.3	0.43
38.8	9.7	43.1	371	6.0	0.63
34.1	8.5	48.7	343	2.4	0.40
14.8	3.7	17.4	295	9.0	0.40
12.7	3.2	14.9	248	7.0	0.30
22.7	5.7	56.7	403	3.6	0.17
21.6	5.4	54.0	355	9.3	0.63
13.7	3.4	35.1	394	4.5	0.13
32.7	8.2	45.4	376	3.8	0.55
25.6	6.4	36.5	377	8.4	0.95
14.4	3.6	38.0	504	12.0	0.50
12.8	3.2	36.5	438	6.1	0.25
14.3	3.6	42.3	417	6.4	0.55
19.5	4.9	29.4	342	4.3	0.30
14.0	3.5	39.6	415	8.1	0.45
13.8	3.5	40.8	414	6.4	0.55
19.4	4.9	29.1	344	4.4	0.35
18.1	4.5	39.0	426	7.8	0.35
13.6	3.4	40.3	414	6.6	0.55
12.7	3.2	41.7	385	5.2	0.38

A *small* cream cake could be a good treat option. Although the saturated fat content is high, you'll often save on sugar compared with other cakes.

CAKES, BREADS
AND PASTRIES **91**

	AN AVERAGE PORTION EQUALS (G):
Mr Kipling, French fancie	1 cake
Mr Kipling, lemon slice	1 cake
Mr Kipling, mini battenberg	1 cake
Mr Kipling, Mississippi mud pie	1 pie
Mr Kipling, rhubarb & custard pie	1 pie
Mr Kipling, Victoria slice	1 cake
Mr Kipling, Viennese whirl	1 whirl
Muffin, blueberry (1 small muffin)	67
Muffins, American, choc chip (1 small muffin)	75
Scones, all butter, sultana (1 scone)	73
Scones, all butter (1 scone)	58
Soreen banana loaf (1 slice)	29
Soreen fruity malt loaf (1 slice)	33
Sponge, fatless, jam filled (1 slice)	60
Victorian sandwich, butter cream and jam (1 slice)	58

Breads and pastries

Bagel, cinnamon and raisin (1 bagel)	85
Bagel, plain (1 bagel)	85
Bagel, wholemeal (1 bagel)	85
Belgian waffle (1 waffle)	25
Brioche (1 roll)	35
Croissant (1 croissant)	44
Crumpet (1 crumpet)	50
Fruit loaf (1 slice)	36
Genius white bread (1 slice)	36
Hot cross bun	70
Hot cross bun, luxury	70
Hovis, best of both (1 slice)	37
Hovis, granary (1 slice)	36
Hovis, original wheatgerm (1 slice)	36
Hovis, Nimble, wholemeal (1 slice)	22

SUGAR PER PORTION (G)	TEASPOONS OF SUGAR PER PORTION	SUGAR PER 100G	ENERGY (KCAL) PER 100G	SATURATES PER 100G	SALT PER 100G
16.5	4.1	59.3	378	4.4	0.58
14.9	3.7	44.1	398	3.3	0.55
22.0	5.5	67.2	453	4.7	0.55
18.3	4.6	34.6	400	5.5	0.33
17.8	4.5	26.9	355	4.9	0.30
11.8	3.0	44.5	443	5.6	0.63
8.4	2.1	30.2	504	10.9	0.60
18.4	4.6	27.5	375	1.3	0.40
21.3	5.3	28.4	385	10.7	0.60
16.9	4.2	23.1	370	8.6	1.27
10.0	2.5	17.2	366	7.3	0.95
6.6	1.6	22.6	313	1.3	0.65
5.7	1.4	17.4	310	0.5	0.72
28.6	7.2	47.7	302	1.6	1.00
17.9	4.5	30.8	396	4.7	0.54
7.1	1.8	8.4	263	0.2	0.80
6.3	1.6	7.4	272	0.2	0.95
4.1	1.0	4.8	248	0.4	0.90
8.0	2.0	32.0	497	18	0.8
4.3	1.1	12.4	350	1.8	1.20
2.6	0.6	5.9	423	15.9	0.75
2.0	0.5	3.9	212	0.2	1.12
8.1	2.0	22.4	285	0.5	0.44
1.6	0.4	4.4	276	0.3	0.90
14.1	3.5	20.1	203	1.2	0.33
17.2	4.3	24.5	295	1.4	0.55
1.5	0.4	4.0	233	0.4	0.86
1.2	0.3	3.4	256	0.7	1.03
1.1	0.3	3.1	224	0.4	0.96
0.5	0.1	2.2	233	0.6	0.93

CAKES, BREADS
AND PASTRIES **93**

	AN AVERAGE PORTION EQUALS (G):
Milk roll (1 slice)	18
Mission multigrain wrap (1 wrap)	61
Muffin, English (1 muffin)	62
Pain au chocolat (1 pain au chocolat)	80
Pitta, white (1 pitta)	60
Pitta, wholemeal (1 pitta)	60
Scotch pancake (1 pancake)	30
Scotch pancake, lemon and raisin (1 pancake)	35
Tea cake (1 tea cake)	63
Tregroes toffee waffle (1 waffle)	35
Waffle, toasting (1 waffle)	25
Warburtons, fruit loaf with orange (1 slice)	35
Warburtons, raisin loaf with cinnamon (1 slice)	36
Warburtons, seeded batch (1 slice)	46
White bread (1 slice)	40
Wholemeal bread (1 slice)	40
Wrap, white tortilla (1 wrap)	64
Wrap, wholegrain tortilla (1 wrap)	64

SUGAR PER PORTION (G)	TEASPOONS OF SUGAR PER PORTION	SUGAR PER 100G	ENERGY (KCAL) PER 100G	SATURATES PER 100G	SALT PER 100G
0.7	0.2	4.0	254	1.3	1.00
2.1	0.5	3.5	309	3.3	1.17
5.1	1.3	8.3	245	0.2	1.00
13.6	3.4	17.0	432	12.8	0.75
2.5	0.6	4.1	269	0.3	0.88
2.9	0.7	4.9	257	0.3	0.83
5.8	1.4	19.2	260	0.4	1.00
10.0	2.5	28.7	269	0.3	0.93
8.9	2.2	14.3	262	0.5	0.75
14.0	3.5	40.4	463	7	0.7
7.4	1.8	29.5	461	10.2	0.80
8.9	2.2	25.5	254	0.4	0.85
8.7	2.2	24.3	273	1.1	0.03
1.5	0.4	3.2	300	1.9	0.98
1.7	0.4	4.2	235	0.4	0.75
2.2	0.5	5.4	232	0.4	0.74
1.6	0.4	2.5	285	0.2	0.93
1.6	0.4	2.5	269	1.9	0.93

CAKES, BREADS
AND PASTRIES

	AN AVERAGE PORTION EQUALS (G):

Desserts

After Eight dessert	70
Alpro Soya, smooth chocolate dessert	125
Alpro Soya, vanilla dessert	125
Angel Delight (¼ pack made with semi-skimmed milk)	92
Bakewell tart (⅙ tart)	88
Bread and butter pudding	125
Cadbury's Desserts, creme egg	70
Cadbury's Desserts, milk chocolate & caramel	70
Cadbury's Desserts, milk chocolate	70
Cadbury's Desserts, white chocolate	70
Cheese cake, fruit	85
Chocolate tart	75
Christmas pudding	100
Crème brûlée	100
Crème caramel	100
Crumble, fruit	125
Egg custard tart	85
Gü, after dark morello cherry bakewell puds	90
Gü, black forest gateau	85
Gü, chocolate & vanilla cheesecakes	90
Gü, chocolate banoffees	85
Gü, chocolate ganache pots	45
Gü, chocolate melting puds	100
Gü, chocolate orange mini puds	45
Gü, chocolate orange pudding	100
Gü, chocolate soufflés	65
Gü, key lime pie	90
Gü, lemon cheesecakes	90
Gü, mango & passionfruit cheesecakes	45
Gü, zillionaires puds	92

* for an explanation of this symbol, see page 16.

SUGAR PER PORTION (G)	TEASPOONS OF SUGAR PER PORTION	SUGAR PER 100G	ENERGY (KCAL) PER 100G	SATURATES PER 100G	SALT PER 100G
16.6	4.2	23.7	178	4.4	0.00
13.1	3.3	10.5	83	0.5	0.14
13.4	3.3	10.7	85	0.4	0.14
11.9	3.0	13.0	117	3.7	0.47
24.9	6.2	28.3	439	8.5	0.43
30.1	7.5	24.1	220	5.3	0.25
23.0	5.8	32.9	230	6.4	0.10
18.2	4.6	26.0	215	*	*
17.2	4.3	24.6	225	*	*
20.9	5.2	29.8	225	*	*
13.3	3.3	15.7	243	2.6	0.63
21.2	5.3	28.3	495	19.1	0.08
40.2	11.6	46.2	219	6.1	0.43
15.3	3.8	15.3	321	17.4	0.10
20.6	5.2	20.6	113	1.2	0.20
30.1	7.5	24.1	220	5.3	0.25
11.7	2.9	13.8	273	5.3	0.14
17.8	4.5	21.5	227	8.2	trace
16.4	4.1	19.3	303	12.5	0.25
19.7	4.9	21.9	404	15.7	0.25
23.8	6.0	28.0	158	14.9	0.25
9.6	2.4	21.0	442	23.1	trace
31.4	7.9	31.4	421	16.3	trace
9.5	2.4	21.2	443	23.1	trace
31.1	7.8	31.1	421	16.2	trace
15.4	3.9	23.7	461	20.6	0.25
19.3	4.8	22.7	370	14.9	0.25
18.7	4.7	20.8	358	12.9	0.50
8.9	2.2	19.8	345	14.9	trace
29.6	7.4	32.3	408	17.3	0.25

If you're watching your weight, sugar-free jelly is the lowest calorie dessert of them all.

DESSERTS,
PUDDINGS AND
ICE CREAM

	AN AVERAGE PORTION EQUALS (G):
Heinz treacle pudding, canned	80
Lemon meringue pie	100
Lemon tart	75
Meringue nest (1 nest)	13
Milky Bar dessert	70
Pancakes, ready made, microwave, (1 pancake)	62
Pie, fruit, pastry top and bottom	110
Rolo Dessert	70
Sponge flan	25
Sponge pudding, chocolate, fresh	110
Sponge pudding, syrup, fresh	110
Spotted dick	110
Treacle tart	100
Trifle, fruit	150
Trifle, sherry, premium range	150

Rice puddings and traditional milk puddings

Ambrosia, creamy macaroni (½ can)	200
Ambrosia, creamy semolina (½ can)	200
Ambrosia, creamy tapioca (½ can)	200
Ambrosia, rice pudding (½ can)	200
Ambrosia, rice pudding, low fat (½ can)	200
Rice Pudding, clotted cream, fresh	125

Rice pudding scores amber for sugar and is a good source of calcium – not a bad choice overall.

Sundaes, mousses and jellies

Aero mousse, milk chocolate	59
Aero mousse, mint chocolate	58
Aero mousse, white chocolate	58
After Eight mousse	57
Hartley's 10 cal fruit flavoured jelly	175
Jelly, made up	125
Jelly, no added sugar, made up	125
Jelly with fruit, made up	175

SUGAR PER PORTION (G)	TEASPOONS OF SUGAR PER PORTION	SUGAR PER 100G	ENERGY (KCAL) PER 100G	SATURATES PER 100G	SALT PER 100G
28.5	7.1	35.6	285	2.8	1.00
46.2	11.6	46.2	219	6.1	0.43
20.6	5.2	27.5	439	17.6	0.13
12.2	3.1	91.1	393	0.1	0.25
13.8	3.4	19.7	231	9.2	0.20
2.3	0.6	3.6	225	5.2	0.73
31.2	7.8	28.4	354	12.8	0.99
17.8	4.5	25.4	243	8.0	0.40
9.3	2.3	37.0	364	1.1	0.73
31.2	7.8	28.4	354	11.5	0.99
52.0	13.0	47.0	350	5.3	0.84
31.2	7.8	28.4	351	8.1	0.25
15.3	3.8	15.3	321	17.4	0.10
24.8	6.2	16.5	155	4.8	0.20
21.2	5.3	14.1	211	8.9	0.20
17.6	4.4	8.8	89	1	0.25
17.6	4.4	8.8	81	1.1	0.25
17.2	4.3	8.6	75	1.1	0.25
19.8	5.0	9.9	107	1.3	0.13
18	4.5	9	81	0.7	0.13
12	3.0	9.8	246	10	0.13
11.4	2.9	19.4	160	3.7	0.20
12.2	3.1	21.1	187	7.3	0.20
11.6	2.9	20.0	170	5.0	0.20
10.0	2.5	17.6	233	11.4	0.10
1.8	0.4	1.0	5	0.0	0.25
23.3	5.8	18.6	80	0.0	0.10
1.3	0.3	1.0	5	0.0	0.14
25.7	6.4	14.7	61	0.0	trace

DESSERTS, PUDDINGS AND ICE CREAM

	AN AVERAGE PORTION EQUALS (G):
Mousse, chocolate, premium range	100
Mousse, chocolate, value range	62
Mousse, chocolate	62
Mousse, lemon	62
Ski mousse, lemon meringue	60
Ski mousse, strawberry	60
Sundae, chocolate	140
Sundae, chocolate, premium range	127
Sundae, strawberry	145

Pot rices

Ambrosia, chocolate rice	120
Ambrosia, Devon custard rice	190
Ambrosia, light rice pudding	115
Ambrosia, original rice	120
Ambrosia, rice apple	120
Ambrosia, rice with strawberry jam on the side	145
Ambrosia, strawberry rice	120
Müller® Rice, apple	190
Müller® Rice, banana & toffee	190
Müller® Rice, chocolate caramel	190
Müller® Rice, original	190

Custards

Ambrosia, Devon custard	150
Ambrosia, low fat Devon custard	150
Custard, fresh, ready-made premium range	125
Custard, fresh, ready-made	125
Custard, made up with semi-skimmed milk	125
Custard, made up with whole milk	125

SUGAR PER PORTION (G)	TEASPOONS OF SUGAR PER PORTION	SUGAR PER 100G	ENERGY (KCAL) PER 100G	SATURATES PER 100G	SALT PER 100G
29.2	7.3	29.2	319	12.3	trace
9.9	2.5	16.0	136	3.7	0.25
13.0	3.3	21.0	185	5.8	0.19
12.7	3.2	20.5	185	7.0	0.20
11.5	2.9	19.1	137	3.3	0.20
9.5	2.4	15.8	131	3.5	0.20
17.9	4.5	12.8	261	10.1	0.13
22.5	5.6	17.7	381	18.6	0.13
26.1	6.5	18.0	226	9.6	0.10
12.2	3.1	10.2	106	1.5	0.12
17.9	4.5	9.4	104	1.5	0.12
9.1	2.3	7.9	86	0.5	0.13
10.8	2.7	9.0	104	1.5	0.13
10.8	2.7	9.0	104	1.5	0.13
24.2	6.1	16.7	124	1.1	0.10
12.2	3.1	10.2	103	1.3	0.15
25.7	6.4	13.5	108	1.3	0.20
25.7	6.4	13.5	109	1.3	0.20
26.8	6.7	14.1	115	1.6	0.20
19.6	4.9	10.3	103	1.5	0.20
17.3	4.3	11.5	100	1.6	trace
11.1	2.8	7.4	89	0.6	trace
15.1	3.8	12.1	197	8.7	trace
12.5	3.1	10.0	119	3.8	trace
14.1	3.5	11.3	95	1.2	0.17
13.8	3.4	11.0	118	2.9	0.17

AN AVERAGE
PORTION EQUALS
(G):

Ice cream and iced desserts

Ben and Jerry's, choc fudge brownie (2 x 50ml scoops)	83
Ben and Jerry's, cookie dough (2 x 50ml scoops)	85
Ben and Jerry's, Greek-style frozen yogurt strawberry shortcake (2 x 50ml scoops)	83
Ben and Jerry's, phish food (2 x 50ml scoops)	86
Calippo, all flavours (1 mini lolly)	80
Carte D'Or geletaria, Eton mess (2 x 50ml scoops)	56
Carte D'Or geletaria, mascarpone (2 x 50ml scoops)	53
Carte D'Or geletaria, rum and raisin (2 x 50ml scoops)	50
Carte D'Or geletaria, vanilla (2 x 50ml scoops)	50
Cornetto, classico (1 from a multi pack)	60
Cornetto, strawberry (1 from a multi pack)	60
Cornish vanilla ice cream (2 x 50ml scoops)	44
Del Monte 100% juice (1 lolly)	75
Fab (1 from a multi pack)	63
Haagen-Daz, Belgian chocolate (2 x 50ml scoops)	89
Haagen-Daz, salted caramel (2 x 50ml scoops)	88
Haagen-Daz, Vanilla (2 x 50ml scoops)	90
Ice cream roll (1 slice)	42
Ice pop (1 ice pop)	45
Jubbly, strawberry (1 Jubbly)	63

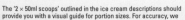

The '2 × 50ml scoops' outlined in the ice cream descriptions should provide you with a visual guide for portion sizes. For accuracy, we

SUGAR PER PORTION (G)	TEASPOONS OF SUGAR PER PORTION	SUGAR PER 100G	ENERGY (KCAL) PER 100G	SATURATES PER 100G	SALT PER 100G
22.4	5.5	27.0	260	8.0	0.23
21.3	5.3	25.0	270	9.0	0.17
17.4	4.3	21.0	200	4.5	0.15
24.0	6.0	28.0	270	8.0	0.17
14.5	3.6	18.0	92	trace	trace
16.0	4.0	27.0	180	5.0	0.11
13.8	3.4	26.0	210	8.0	0.11
11.0	2.8	22.0	200	5.0	0.14
11.5	2.9	23.0	200	7.0	0.15
14.0	3.5	23.0	320	14.0	0.23
17.0	4.3	29.0	280	10.0	0.18
8.3	2.1	18.9	170	4.8	0.18
14.5	3.6	19.3	86	trace	trace
14.2	3.6	22.6	141	2.2	0.01
19.4	4.9	21.8	313	12.4	0.20
19.8	5.0	22.5	284	11.1	0.50
12.9	3.2	14.3	251	10.4	0.20
11.4	2.8	27.2	212	2.8	0.25
3.2	0.8	7.0	28	trace	trace
4.0	1.0	6.4	27	trace	trace

have also listed the average portion sizes for ice cream in grams.

The two 50ml scoops that most tubs of ice cream recommend as a serving, and which we've used here as a visual guide, is quite small. Eat much more than this and many of the ambers will turn red!

	AN AVERAGE PORTION EQUALS (G):
Magnum, almond (1 from a multi pack)	82
Magnum, classic (1 from a multi pack)	79
Magnum, white (1 from a multi pack)	79
Mini Milk (1 lolly)	23
Mint choc chip ice cream (2 x 50ml scoops)	44
Neapolitan ice cream (2 x 50ml scoops)	43
Ribena ice lollies (1 lolly)	75
Rocket lollies (1 from a multi pack)	63
Sorbet, lemon (2 x 50ml scoops)	78
Sorbet, mango (2 x 50ml scoops)	79
Sorbet, raspberry (2 x 50ml scoops)	77
Twister (1 x 50ml mini lolly)	39
Vanilla soft scoop ice cream (2 x 50ml scoops)	42
Viennetta, mint (⅛th of a dessert)	53
Viennetta, strawberry (⅛th of a dessert)	54
Viennetta, vanilla (⅛th of a dessert)	53
Weight Watchers, toffee with fudge pieces (1 x 100ml individual pot)	55

SUGAR PER PORTION (G)	TEASPOONS OF SUGAR PER PORTION	SUGAR PER 100G	ENERGY (KCAL) PER 100G	SATURATES PER 100G	SALT PER 100G
24.0	6.0	29.0	330	13.0	0.15
21.0	5.3	27.0	310	14.0	0.13
24.0	6.0	31.0	300	12.0	0.17
4.6	1.2	20.0	135	2.0	0.16
9.2	2.3	20.8	183	6.0	0.17
8.2	2.0	19.0	164	5.1	0.15
11.9	3.0	15.9	67	trace	trace
10.6	2.6	16.8	75	trace	0.22
20.4	5.1	26.1	122	0.1	trace
24.0	6.0	30.4	133	0.1	trace
17.9	4.5	23.2	105	0.0	trace
7.0	1.8	18.0	112	1.5	0.04
8.1	2.1	19.4	165	5.6	0.14
10.6	2.7	20.0	250	14.0	0.14
10.8	2.7	20.0	240	13.0	0.13
11.1	2.7	21.0	250	13.0	0.12
9.8	2.5	17.9	139	1.7	0.10

	AN AVERAGE PORTION EQUALS (G):
Cheese, spreads and cream	
Butter	10
Cheddar	30
Cream, double	1 tbsp
Dairylea	25
Philadelphia	30
Philadelphia, extra light	30
Philadelphia, light	30
Processed cheese slices (1 slice)	17
Wensleydale, apricot	30
Wensleydale, cranberries	30
Yogurts	
Activia, lemon & lime	125
Activia, pineapple & coconut	125
Activia 0% Fat, cherry	125
Activia 0% Fat, forest fruit	125
Activia 0% Fat, mixed red fruits	125
Activia 0% Fat, mixed yellow fruits	125
Activia 0% Fat, peach	125
Alpro Soya, alternative to yogurt, blueberry	125
Alpro Soya, simply plain	150
Danio strained yogurt, fruit	160
Danio strained yogurt, natural	150
Frubes pouches	40
Greek-style yogurt	150
Low-fat fruit yogurt	125
Low-fat fruit yogurt, value range	125
Müller® Amore®	120
Müller® Crunch Corner® banana chocolate flakes	135
Müller® Crunch Corner® milk chocolate digestive	135

Natural cheese contains barely any sugar so we haven't listed very many. But watch out for the sugar in cream and processed cheese as well as in those with added dried fruits.

SUGAR PER PORTION (G)	TEASPOONS OF SUGAR PER PORTION	SUGAR PER 100G	ENERGY (KCAL) PER 100G	SATURATES PER 100G	SALT PER 100G
trace	0.0	trace	742	51.0	1.2
trace	0.0	trace	410	21.7	1.7
0.4	0.1	2.6	445	29.7	trace
1.4	1.6	5.5	230	11.5	1.5
1.0	0.2	3.2	245	14.0	1.0
1.7	0.4	5.5	98	2.1	0.9
1.2	0.3	4.0	156	7.6	1.0
0.7	0.2	4.3	269	9.7	2.0
4.5	1.1	15.0	345	15.0	1.0
2.6	0.7	8.8	374	16.9	1.8
8.4	2.1	6.7	55	trace	0.20
16.8	4.2	13.4	100	2.5	0.10
11.6	2.9	9.3	60	trace	0.30
10.5	2.6	8.4	58	trace	0.30
10.5	2.6	8.4	58	trace	0.30
9.5	2.4	7.6	55	trace	0.20
11.1	2.8	8.9	57	trace	0.20
12.1	3.0	9.7	75	0.4	0.21
3.2	0.8	2.1	50	0.4	0.25
18.2	4.6	11.4	82	0.1	0.10
5.1	1.3	3.4	54	0.0	0.10
5.8	1.5	14.5	105	1.9	0.10
7.7	1.9	5.1	120	0.2	6.00
17.6	4.4	14.1	87	0.8	0.15
17.3	4.3	13.8	86	0.8	0.18
18.6	4.7	15.5	158	5.9	0.10
22.7	5.7	16.8	143	3.2	0.25
23.6	5.9	17.5	155	3.4	0.25

	AN AVERAGE PORTION EQUALS (G):
Müller® Crunch Corner® strawberry shortcake	135
Müller® Crunch Corner® toffee hoops	135
Müller® Crunch Corner® vanilla chocolate balls	135
Müller® Fruit Corner® blackberry & raspberry	150
Müller® Fruit Corner® cherry	150
Müller® Fruit Corner® peach & apricot	150
Müller® Fruit Corner® strawberry	150
Müller® Kids Corner® blast off	135
Müllerlight®, average	175
Munch Bunch, double up fromage frais	85
Munch Bunch, fruit yogurt	100
Munch Bunch, strawberry delight jelly	85
Onken, fat free, fruit	150
Onken, fruit	150
Onken, peach, wholegrain	150
Onken, summer fruits, wholegrain	150
Rachel's organic fat free, fruit	150
Rachel's organic low fat, fruit	150
Reduced fat Greek-style yogurt	150
Shape, dessert chocolate	110
Shape, vanilla chocolate sprinkle	120
Shape, zero % fat, fruit	120
Supermarket, premium, cream, fruit	150
Total 0% fat Greek yogurt	170
Weight Watchers, fat free, citrus fruit	120
Weight Watchers, fat free, dessert recipe	120
Weight Watchers, fat free, summer fruits	120
Weight Watchers, Greek-style fat free, coconut	100

SUGAR PER PORTION (G)	TEASPOONS OF SUGAR PER PORTION	SUGAR PER 100G	ENERGY (KCAL) PER 100G	SATURATES PER 100G	SALT PER 100G
23.6	5.9	17.5	157	3.4	0.25
25.5	6.4	18.9	153	3.5	0.25
24.6	6.1	18.2	149	3.4	0.25
19.8	5.0	13.2	105	2.4	0.25
19.7	4.9	13.1	105	2.4	0.25
20.3	5.1	13.5	107	2.4	0.25
22.4	5.6	14.9	112	2.4	0.25
23.6	5.9	17.5	146	4.0	0.30
12.6	3.2	7.2	53	0.1	0.25
12.1	3.0	14.2	110	1.9	0.10
12.4	3.1	12.4	98	1.9	0.20
11.2	2.8	13.2	86	1.1	0.10
19.2	4.8	12.8	79	0.1	0.18
22.2	5.6	14.8	107	1.7	0.20
21.2	5.3	14.1	113	1.7	0.18
21.3	5.3	14.2	111	1.7	0.20
21.6	5.4	14.4	80	0.1	0.18
20.0	5.0	13.3	84	1.0	0.13
12.2	3.0	8.1	79	1.7	0.23
14.9	3.7	13.5	100	1.6	0.10
12.1	3.0	10.1	70	0.1	0.30
10.8	2.7	9.0	64	0.1	0.30
17.6	4.4	11.7	128	4.3	0.10
6.8	1.7	4.0	57	0.0	trace
6.2	1.6	5.2	45	0.1	0.30
7.8	2.0	6.5	49	0.1	0.20
6.6	1.7	5.5	45	0.1	0.10
12.6	3.2	12.6	84	0.4	0.13

Low-fat yogurts can be quite high in sugar. A healthier and less sugary alternative would be natural yogurt topped with a small handful of raspberries.

	AN AVERAGE PORTION EQUALS (G):
Weight Watchers, Greek-Style fat free, strawberry	100
Weight Watchers, Greek-Style fat free, zesty lemon	100
Yop yogurt drink, all flavours (½ bottle)	250

Yogurt breakfast pots (g)

Activia Breakfast Pot, honey yogurt	160
Activia Breakfast Pot, peach yogurt	160
Activia Breakfast Pot, vanilla yogurt	160
Onken muesli pot, all flavours	200

Milk and shakes (ml)

Frijj, chocolate (½ bottle)	235
Frijj, fudge brownie (½ bottle)	235
Frijj, supreme, honeycomb (½ bottle)	235
Mars milkshake	200
Milk, 1%	200
Milk, semi-skimmed milk	200
Milk, skimmed	200
Milk, whole	200
Milkshake, banana	200
Milkshake, chocolate	200
Milkshake, strawberry	200

Probiotics and functional yogurt drinks (g)

Actimel yogurt drink, blueberry (1 pot)	100
Actimel yogurt drink, coconut (1 pot)	100
Actimel yogurt drink, mango & passionfruit (1 pot)	100
Actimel yogurt drink, multi fruit (1 pot)	100
Actimel yogurt drink, original (1 pot)	100
Actimel yogurt drink, raspberry or strawberry (1 pot)	100

SUGAR PER PORTION (G)	TEASPOONS OF SUGAR PER PORTION	SUGAR PER 100G	ENERGY (KCAL) PER 100G	SATURATES PER 100G	SALT PER 100G
12.1	3.0	12.1	77	0.1	0.13
12.6	3.2	12.6	79	0.1	0.14
30.0	7.5	12.0	76	0.9	0.11
21.6	5.4	13.5	120	1.1	0.30
21.3	5.3	13.3	119	1.1	0.30
21.3	5.3	13.3	119	1.1	0.30
26.0	6.5	13.0	110	1.2	0.08
25.4	6.3	10.8	73	0.7	0.20
30.3	7.6	12.9	78	0.7	0.20
27.7	6.9	11.8	88	1.6	0.20
27.0	6.8	13.5	80	1.0	0.17
9.8	2.5	4.9	43	0.7	0.11
9.2	2.3	4.6	48	1.1	0.10
9.4	2.4	4.7	36	trace	0.13
9.0	2.3	4.5	67	2.6	0.10
20.2	5.1	10.1	71	1.1	0.12
21.0	5.3	10.5	76	1.2	0.14
19.4	4.9	9.7	70	1.1	0.12
11.6	2.9	11.6	75	1.1	0.10
12.0	3.0	12.0	80	1.4	0.10
11.6	2.9	11.6	72	1.1	0.10
12.3	3.1	12.3	77	1.1	0.10
10.5	2.6	10.5	71	1.1	0.10
11.6	2.9	11.6	75	1.1	0.10

	AN AVERAGE PORTION EQUALS (G/ML):
Actimel yogurt drink, strawberry & banana (1 pot)	100
Actimel yogurt drink 0.1% fat, original (1 pot)	100
Actimel yogurt drink 0.1% fat, raspberry (1 pot)	100
Benecol Plus Bone Health (1 pot)	68
Benecol, all flavours (1 pot)	68
Yakult (1 pot)	65ml
Yakult Light (1 pot)	65ml

Dairy alternatives (ml)

Almond Breeze chocolate	200
Almond Breeze original	200
Almond Breeze unsweetened	200
Alpro almond	200
Alpro almond, unsweetened	200
Alpro coconut	200
Alpro hazelnut	200
Alpro oat long life	200
Alpro rice light long life	200
Alpro rice long life	200
Alpro soya unsweetened	200
Alpro soya vanilla long life	200
EcoMil almond long life	200
Isola Bio rice/almond long life	200
Oatly chocolate long life	200
Oatly	200
Provamel organic soya unsweetened long life	200
Rice Dream hazelnut/almond drink long life	200
Rice Dream long life	200
Rice Dream vanilla long life	200

All items are fresh and refrigerated unless specified as long life.

SUGAR PER PORTION (G)	TEASPOONS OF SUGAR PER PORTION	SUGAR PER 100G/ML	ENERGY (KCAL) PER 100G/ML	SATURATES PER 100G/ML	SALT PER 100G/ML
11.7	2.9	11.7	75	1.1	0.10
3.3	0.8	3.3	28	trace	0.10
3.5	0.9	3.5	31	trace	0.10
4.3	1.1	6.3	53	0.1	0.10
4.1	1.0	6.0	53	0.1	0.10
9.2	2.3	14.2	66	trace	0.05
3.6	0.9	5.6	42	trace	0.05
16.8	4.2	8.4	48	0.1	0.13
5.6	1.4	2.8	24	trace	0.13
0.1	0.0	0.2	14	trace	0.13
6.0	1.5	3.0	24	0.1	0.10
0.2	0.1	0.1	13	0.1	0.10
3.8	1.0	1.9	20	0.9	0.13
6.0	1.5	3.0	29	0.2	0.13
6.6	1.7	3.3	42	0.1	0.10
4.8	1.2	2.4	33	0.1	0.09
6.6	1.7	3.3	47	0.0	0.09
0.2	0.1	0.1	32	trace	0.03
13.2	3.3	6.6	55	0.3	0.14
7.6	1.9	3.8	46	0.2	0.25
15.0	3.8	7.5	90	0.5	0.10
14.0	3.5	7.0	55	0.2	0.15
8.0	2.0	4.0	35	0.1	0.10
0.2	0.1	0.1	35	0.4	trace
14.2	3.6	7.1	79	0.2	0.10
8.0	2.0	4.0	47	0.1	0.10
9.2	2.3	4.6	511	0.1	0.10

DAIRY PRODUCTS 113

For branded coffees, milks suggested are the standard ones used.

Coffees and hot drinks, branded	AN AVERAGE PORTION EQUALS (ML):
Costa, caffé latte, whole milk (medio)	354
Costa, caffé caramella, whole milk (medio)	354
Costa, chai latte, whole milk (medio)	354
Costa, hot chocolate, whole milk (medio)	354
Costa, hot spiced apple (medio)	354
Costa, mocha latte, whole milk (medio)	354
Costa, mocha, whole milk (medio)	354
Costa, sugar-free caramel latte, whole milk (medio)	354
Starbucks, bar mocha syrup (1 pump)	17g
Starbucks, caffé mocha with whipped cream (tall)	354
Starbucks, caramel frappuccino with whipped cream (tall)	354
Starbucks, caramel macchiato (tall)	354
Starbucks, classic hot choc with whipped cream (tall)	354
Starbucks, coffee frappuccino, no whip (tall)	354
Starbucks, flavoured syrup (1 pump)	10g
Starbucks, mocha frappuccino with whipped cream (tall)	354
Starbucks, semi-skimmed cappuccino (tall)	354
Starbucks, semi-skimmed latte (tall)	354
Starbucks, signature hot choc with whipped cream (tall)	354
Starbucks, white choc mocha with whipped cream (tall)	354
Starbucks, whole milk flat white (short)	236

Per 100ml info has had to be estimated for Starbucks and Costa and may vary depending on exact amount barister pours into your cup.

SUGAR PER PORTION (G)	TEASPOONS OF SUGAR PER PORTION	SUGAR PER 100ML	ENERGY (KCAL) PER 100ML	SATURATES PER 100ML	SALT PER 100ML
14.7	3.7	4.1	56	2.0	*
28.0	7.0	8.0	69	1.7	*
49.3	12.3	13.6	119	2.1	*
34.8	8.7	9.8	90	2.3	*
41.1	10.3	11.7	51	0.0	*
37.7	9.4	10.5	98	2.4	*
34.4	8.6	9.5	86	2.0	*
15.1	3.8	4.3	59	2.0	*
4.8	1.2	28.2	153	trace	*
26.2	6.5	7.4	77	2.2	*
44.1	11.0	12.5	81	1.8	*
25.5	6.4	7.2	59	0.9	*
25.4	6.3	7.2	74	2.0	*
35.4	8.9	10.0	48	0.3	*
4.9	1.2	49.0	200	0.0	*
39.6	9.9	11.2	75	1.8	*
8.1	2.0	2.3	27	0.5	*
8.5	2.1	2.4	40	0.7	*
36.4	9.1	10.3	118	4.2	*
44.3	11.1	12.5	91	2.6	*
8.0	2.0	3.4	50	1.4	*

A plain latte made with lower fat milk is one of the better coffee options as it's low sugar and a great supplier of calcium.

* for an explanation of this symbol, see page 16.

	AN AVERAGE PORTION EQUALS (ML):
Hot drinks general	
Bovril meat stock drink	12
Cocoa, with whole milk	250
Cocoa, with semi-skimmed milk	250
Cocoa, with skimmed milk	250
Coffee, filter, no milk	250
Coffee, instant, with semi-skimmed milk	250
Espresso	single shot
Fruit tea	200
Herbal tea	200
Horlicks, Light Malt, made with water	200
Horlicks, Traditional Malt, made with semi-skimmed milk	200
Hot Chocolate, Instant, made with water	200
Hot chocolate, low calorie, (11g sachet made up)	200
Hot Chocolate, made with semi-skimmed milk	200
Lift reduced sweetness instant lemon tea (7g powder)	200
Ovaltine, Chocolate, made with semi-skimmed milk	200
Ovaltine, Chocolate, made with water	200
Ovaltine, Original Light, made with water	200
Ovaltine, Original, made with semi-skimmed milk	200
Tea with semi-skimmed milk	250
Soft drinks	
7Up (1 can)	330
Appletiser	250
Belvoir, Coconut and lime presse	250
Belvoir, Elderflower presse	200

SUGAR PER PORTION (G)	TEASPOONS OF SUGAR PER PORTION	SUGAR PER 100ML	ENERGY (KCAL) PER 100ML	SATURATES PER 100ML	SALT PER 100ML
0.2	0.0	1.6	178	0.3	11.50
17.0	4.3	6.8	76	2.6	0.15
18.0	4.5	7.2	57	1.2	0.15
18.0	4.5	7.2	44	0.3	0.15
0.0	0.0	0.0	trace	0.0	trace
1.8	0.4	0.7	7	0.1	trace
trace	0.0	trace	3	trace	trace
trace	0.0	trace	1	trace	trace
trace	0.0	trace	1	trace	trace
15.8	4.0	7.9	59	0.3	0.25
20.8	5.2	10.4	94	1.4	0.25
16.6	4.2	8.3	58	1.2	0.28
3.5	0.9	1.8	20	0.5	0.19
22.1	5.5	11.1	80	1.4	0.19
5.5	1.4	2.8	12	trace	trace
23.1	5.8	11.6	96	1.3	0.15
10.5	2.6	5.3	38	0.5	0.02
9.3	2.3	4.7	51	1.0	0.20
22.2	5.6	11.1	97	1.2	0.15
1.8	0.5	0.7	7	0.1	trace
37.0	9.2	11.2	43	0.0	trace
25.5	6.4	10.2	47	0.0	0.00
20.0	5.0	8.0	32	trace	trace
20.0	5.0	10.0	40	0.0	0.00

Beware: ginger beer is often even more sugary than cola.

	AN AVERAGE PORTION EQUALS (ML):
Belvoir, Fresh Root Ginger Beer	250
Belvoir, Raspberry Lemonade (1 can)	250
Bottlegreen elderflower pressé	200
Coca Cola (1 can)	330
Coca Cola Cherry (1 can)	330
Cola, Full Sugar (1 can)	330
Dr Pepper (1 can)	330
Fentimans ginger beer (1 bottle)	275
Fizzy drink, diet, any flavour (1 can)	330
Fruit Shoot (1 bottle)	200
Fruit Shoot Hydro (1 bottle)	350
Fruit Shoot, low sugar, apple and blackcurrant (1 bottle)	200
Ginger beer	250
Iron Bru	250
J20, apple and mango (1 bottle)	275
J20, apple and raspberry (1 bottle)	275
J20, orange and passion fruit (1 bottle)	275
Koji sparkling fruit infusion, all flavours (1 bottle)	330
Lemonade, cloudy, average	250
Lemonade, full sugar, average	250
Lemonade, pink, zero, average	250
Lemonade, value, diet, average	250
Lilt (1 can)	330
Lipton ice tea, all flavours (1 bottle)	500
Lorina traditional pink lemonade	250
Oasis, all flavours (1 bottle)	500
Old Jamaica, Ginger Beer (1 can)	330
Orangina (1 can)	330
Pepsi Cola (1 can)	330
Pepsi Max (1 can)	330
Ribena Plus, Immunity (1 carton)	200
Ribena ready to drink, full sugar (1 carton)	200

SUGAR PER PORTION (G)	TEASPOONS OF SUGAR PER PORTION	SUGAR PER 100ML	ENERGY (KCAL) PER 100ML	SATURATES PER 100ML	SALT PER 100ML
24.5	6.1	9.8	39	trace	trace
27.3	6.8	10.9	44	0.0	trace
14.6	3.7	7.3	29	0.0	trace
35.0	8.7	10.6	42	0.0	0.00
37.0	9.2	11.2	45	0.0	0.00
35.6	8.9	10.8	43	trace	trace
34.0	8.5	10.3	42	0.0	trace
25.9	6.5	9.4	38	0.0	0.00
0.0	0.0	0.0	1	0.0	0.00
21.0	5.3	10.5	45	0.0	0.00
0.0	0.0	0.0	1	0.0	0.00
1.6	0.4	0.8	5	0.0	trace
34.3	8.6	13.7	55	trace	trace
26.3	6.6	10.5	43	trace	trace
17.1	4.3	6.2	27	trace	trace
20.1	5.0	7.3	32	trace	trace
19.8	5.0	7.2	32	trace	nil
10.9	2.7	3.3	15	trace	trace
33.8	8.4	13.5	56	0.0	trace
28.8	7.2	11.5	47	trace	trace
0.8	0.2	0.3	5	trace	trace
trace	0.0	trace	1	trace	trace
15.2	3.8	4.6	20	0.0	0.00
34.5	8.6	6.9	28	nil	trace
32.0	8.0	12.8	53	0.0	0.00
20.5	5.1	4.1	17	0.0	trace
52.8	13.2	16.0	64	0.0	0.00
33.7	8.4	10.2	42	0.0	0.00
35.0	8.7	10.6	43	0.0	0.00
trace	0.0	trace	0	0.0	0.00
2.0	0.5	1.0	5	trace	trace
21.2	5.3	10.6	43	0	trace

'Full sugar' lemonade may seem lower sugar than other similar fizzy drinks, but this is because many brands contain a combination of sugar and sweeteners.

	AN AVERAGE PORTION EQUALS (ML):
R Whites lemonade (1 can)	330
San Pellegrino, all flavours (1 can)	330
Schloer, all flavours	250
Schweppes lemonade (1 can)	330
Sprite (1 can)	330
Squash, high juice, full sugar, all flavours	250
Squash, high juice, no added sugar, all flavours	250
Squash, no added sugar	250
Tango, apple (1 can)	330
Tango, orange (1 can)	330

Fruit juices and smoothies

Apple juice, from concentrate	200
Apple juice, not from concentrate	200
Cranberry juice drink, 10% juice	200
Happy Monkey Kids Smoothie, orange and mango	180
Innocent Extra Juicy Smoothie, cherries and strawberries	250
Innocent Kids Smoothie, apples and blackcurrants	180
Innocent Kids Smoothie, strawberries, blackberries and raspberries	180
Innocent Smoothie, kiwis, apples and limes	250
Innocent Smoothie, mangoes and passionfruits	250
Innocent Smoothie, pomegranate, blueberry and acai	250
Innocent Super Smoothie Defence	360
Lemon juice	5
My-5 fruit shoot	200

SUGAR PER PORTION (G)	TEASPOONS OF SUGAR PER PORTION	SUGAR PER 100ML	ENERGY (KCAL) PER 100ML	SATURATES PER 100ML	SALT PER 100ML
7.9	2.0	2.4	11	0.0	trace
32.0	8.0	9.7	43	0.0	0.00
28.8	7.2	11.5	49	trace	trace
14.0	3.5	4.2	18	0.0	trace
21.8	5.4	6.6	28	0.0	trace
20.0	5.0	8.0	37	trace	trace
1.8	0.4	0.7	4	trace	trace
0.5	0.1	0.2	1	trace	trace
6.9	1.7	2.1	10	0.0	trace
14.2	3.5	4.3	19	0.0	trace
20.6	5.2	10.3	44	0.0	0.00
20.6	5.2	10.3	46	0.0	0.00
23.8	6.0	11.9	49	trace	trace
21.8	5.4	12.1	54	trace	trace
28.3	7.1	11.3	57	0.1	trace
22.0	5.5	12.2	55	trace	trace
16.9	4.2	9.4	50	trace	trace
25.5	6.4	10.2	50	0.1	0.03
27.3	6.8	10.9	53	0.1	0.03
34.8	8.7	13.9	63	0.1	trace
50.4	12.6	14.0	64	0.2	trace
trace	0.0	1.6	7	0.0	0.00
16.4	4.1	8.2	36	trace	0.0

Smoothies are a great way to get children to eat more fruit, but they can contain as much sugar as fizzy drinks, so should be given as an occasional treat.

	AN AVERAGE PORTION EQUALS (ML):
Ocean Spray, 25% juice drink, light,	200
Ocean Spray, 25% juice drink	200
Orange juice, from concentrate	200
Orange juice, not from concentrate	200
Pineapple juice, from concentrate	200
Pineapple, banana and coconut Smoothie	250
Pomegranate juice drink	250
Strawberry and banana smoothie	250
Tomato juice, from concentrate	200

Flavoured waters

Flavoured water, no added sugar	250
V Water, so be	500
Vitamin water (1 bottle)	500
Volvic, touch of fruit	500
Volvic, touch of fruit, sugar free	500

Sports and energy drinks

Gatorade Recover	500
Gatorade, all flavours	500
Lucozade Energy, all flavours	500
Lucozade Sport, all flavours	500
Lucozade Sport, Lite, all flavours	500
Maxinutrition protein milk, strawberry	250
Mountain Dew Energy, full sugar	500
Nurishment Active, chocolate	500
Powerade, all flavours	500
Red Bull, all flavours	250
Red Bull, sugar free	250
Red Bull, zero	250
Relentless energy drink	250

SUGAR PER PORTION (G)	TEASPOONS OF SUGAR PER PORTION	SUGAR PER 100ML	ENERGY (KCAL) PER 100ML	SATURATES PER 100ML	SALT PER 100ML
2.8	0.7	1.4	8	0.0	0.0
23.2	5.8	11.6	49	0.0	trace
21.0	5.3	10.5	47	0.0	0.00
20.0	5.0	10.0	48	0.0	0.00
22.0	5.5	11.0	48	0.0	0.00
29.8	7.4	11.9	68	1.2	trace
30.3	6.1	12.1	53	trace	0.0
27.5	6.9	11.0	49	trace	trace
6.1	1.5	3.1	19	0.0	0.00
trace	0.0	trace	2	trace	trace
0.0	0.0	0.0	2	trace	0.00
15.0	3.8	3.0	13	0.0	0.00
25	6	4.8	20	0.0	trace
0.0	0.0	0.0	1	0.0	0.00
13.0	3.3	2.6	25	trace	0.12
30.0	7.5	6.0	25	0.0	0.13
86.0	21.5	17.2	70	0.0	trace
17.5	17.5	3.5	28	0.0	trace
5.0	1.3	1.0	10	0.0	trace
11.8	2.9	4.7	52	0.1	trace
60.0	15.0	12.0	48	0.0	0.00
53.0	13.3	10.6	93	0.9	0.15
19.5	4.9	3.9	17	0.0	0.13
27.5	6.9	11.0	45	0.0	0.10
2.5	0.6	1.0	3	0.0	0.20
0.0	0.0	0.0	0	0.0	0.20
25.3	6.3	10.1	44	0.0	0.13

	AN AVERAGE PORTION EQUALS (ML):
Burger King	
Caramel Frappé (regular)	400
Caramel Frappé (large)	500
Chocolate Frappé (regular)	400
Chocolate Frappé (large)	500
Chocolate Shake (regular)	400
Chocolate Shake (large)	500
Strawberry Banana Smoothie (regular)	400
Strawberry Banana Smoothie (large)	500
Strawberry Shake (regular)	400
Strawberry Shake (large)	500
Tropical Mango Smoothie (regular)	400
Tropical Mango Smoothie (large)	500
Vanilla Shake (regular)	400
Vanilla Shake (large)	500
KFC	
KFC Krushems® Maltesers	1 Krushems®
KFC Krushems® Twix	1 Krushems®
McDonalds	
Banana Milkshake (medium)	400
Banana Milkshake (large)	500
Chocolate Milkshake (medium)	400
Chocolate Milkshake (large)	500
Fruitizz (small)	250
Fruitizz (medium)	400
Fruitizz (large)	500
Strawberry & Banana Smoothie (medium)	400
Strawberry & Banana Smoothie (large)	500
Strawberry Milkshake (medium)	400
Strawberry Milkshake (large)	500
Vanilla Milkshake (medium)	400
Vanilla Milkshake (large)	500

SUGAR PER PORTION (G)	TEASPOONS OF SUGAR PER PORTION	SUGAR PER 100ML	ENERGY (KCAL) PER 100ML	SATURATES PER 100ML	SALT PER 100ML
36.3	9.1	9.1	85	1.2	0.10
45.8	11.5	9.2	84	1.0	0.10
44.6	11.2	11.2	82	1.2	0.06
57.2	14.3	11.4	82	1.0	0.07
74.0	18.5	18.5	112	1.9	0.18
102.4	25.6	20.5	122	1.9	0.19
45.3	11.3	11.3	52	0.1	trace
60.9	15.2	12.2	56	0.0	trace
72.1	18.0	18.0	108	1.9	0.17
98.7	24.7	19.7	117	1.8	0.17
49.6	12.4	12.4	55	0.1	trace
66.0	16.5	13.2	59	0.1	trace
59.4	14.9	14.9	93	1.9	0.16
73.6	18.4	14.7	92	1.8	0.16
34.6	8.7	21.4	189	3.7	0.33
42.8	10.7	24.3	213	4.7	0.27
63.0	15.8	15.8	98	1.3	0.10
81.0	20.3	15.8	98	1.3	0.10
52.0	13.0	13.0	98	1.3	0.18
67.0	16.8	13.0	98	1.3	0.18
25.0	6.3	10.0	40	0.0	trace
39.0	9.8	10.0	40	0.0	trace
49.0	12.3	10.0	40	0.0	trace
42.0	10.5	10.5	48	0.0	0.08
53.0	13.3	10.5	48	0.0	0.08
62.0	15.5	15.5	95	2.0	0.16
79.0	19.8	15.5	95	2.0	0.16
64.0	16.0	16.0	98	1.3	0.10
81.0	20.3	16.0	98	1.3	0.10

ABV (alcohol by volume) is a standard measure of how much alcohol (ethanol) is contained in an alcoholic drink (the higher the ABV the more alcoholic the drink).

	AN AVERAGE PORTION EQUALS (ML):
Alcoholic drinks	
Alcopop (1 bottle)	275
Archers Aqua (1 bottle)	275
Beer, bitter (1 pint)	568
Brandy (single measure)	25
Brown ale, bottled (1 bottle)	550
Bulmers original cider (1 pint)	568
Croft original sherry	100
Famous Grouse (single measure)	35
Gin with diet tonic	250
Gin (single measure)	25
Gordon's gin & Schweppes tonic (can)	250
Guinness (1 pint)	568
Irish cream (double measure)	50
Lager, premium (1 pint)	568
Lager, standard (1 pint)	568
Liqueur, 20–24% ABV (double measure)	50
Liqueur, 35–40% ABV (double measure)	50
Port	100
Red wine, 12.5–14.5% ABV	175
Rum (single measure)	25
Sherry, dry	100
Sherry, sweet	100
Stella Artois (1 bottle)	660
Strong ale (1 bottle)	500
Vermouth, dry (single measure)	25
Vermouth, sweet (single measure)	25
Vintage cider, 8% ABV	568
Vodka (single measure)	25
Whisky (single measure)	25
White wine, dry, 12–12.5% ABV	175
White wine, medium, 11.5–13.5% ABV,	175
White wine, sparkling	125
White wine, sweet	125

SUGAR PER PORTION (G)	TEASPOONS OF SUGAR PER PORTION	SUGAR PER 100ML	ENERGY (KCAL) PER 100ML	SATURATES PER 100ML	SALT PER 100ML
13.8	3.4	5.0	73	0.0	trace
14.0	3.5	5.1	75	0.0	trace
12.5	3.1	2.2	30	0.0	trace
trace	0.0	trace	220	0.0	trace
16.5	4.1	3.0	30	0.0	trace
20.4	5.1	3.6	41	0.0	trace
9.5	2.4	9.5	145	0.0	trace
trace	0.0	trace	225	0.0	trace
trace	0.0	trace	36	0.0	trace
trace	0.0	trace	222	0.0	trace
14.0	3.5	5.6	58	0.0	trace
8.5	2.1	1.5	30	0.0	trace
10.5	2.6	21.0	305	7.6	0.25
13.6	3.4	2.4	59	0.0	trace
trace	0.0	trace	29	0.0	trace
16.4	4.1	32.8	262	0.0	trace
12.2	3.1	24.4	314	0.0	trace
12.0	3.0	12.0	157	0.0	trace
0.4	0.1	0.2	70	0.0	trace
trace	0.0	trace	222	0.0	trace
1.4	0.4	1.4	116	0.0	trace
6.9	1.7	6.9	135	0.0	trace
trace	0.0	trace	45	0.0	trace
30.5	7.6	6.1	66	0.0	trace
0.8	0.2	3.0	109	0.0	trace
4.0	1.0	15.9	151	0.0	trace
28.4	7.1	5.0	60	0.0	trace
trace	0.0	trace	222	0.0	trace
trace	0.0	trace	222	0.0	trace
1.1	0.3	0.6	65	0.0	trace
5.3	1.3	3.0	75	0.0	trace
3.8	0.9	3.0	75	0.0	trace
12.5	3.1	10.0	120	0.0	trace

Remember, adding non-diet mixers to spirits will affect the sugar content of your favourite tipple.

Getty Images Andrew Bret Wallis 14. **Octopus Publishing Group** 90–95 above right; Sally Scott 96–105 below right; Stephen Conroy 40–46 above left, 40–46 above right, 96–105 above right; Will Heap 15. **Shutterstock** baibaz 46–49 below right; bitt24 56–63 above right; caldix 50–55 below left; CGissemann 36–39 below left; denio109 40–45 below left; Dream79 30–35 above right; Elina Manninen 30–35 above left; Iura_Atom 65 below right; James Clarke 90–95 below right; Jiri Hera 46–49 below left; joannawnuk 50–55 above right; Joe Gough 70–79 below left; Liv Friis-Larsen 114–127 above left; MaraZe 30–35 below right, 80–83 below left; Marco Mayer 86–89 above right; margouillat photo 106–113 below left; Marie C Fields 90–95 below left; Mariyana M 114–127 above right; matin 64 above left; Olga Miltsova 30–35 below left; Palle Christensen 106–113 above left; Piyato 40–45 below right; ScriptX 50–55 below right; Silviu Matei 86–89 below left; svry 70–79 above right; TAGSTOCK1 80–83 above right; Tommaso Lizzul 70–79 above left; V. J. Matthew 65 above right; vanillaechoes 64 below left; Yeko Photo Studio 46–49 above right; Yulia Davidovich 80–83 above left. **Thinkstock** aaa187 70–79 below right; Alexandra Grablewski 36–39 above right; AnjelaGr 84 below left; arinahabich 106–113 below right; bhofack2 114–127 below left; Catherine Eckert 50–55 above left; digicomphoto 84 above left; Easy_Company 114–127 below right; Edi_Eco 18–29 below left; Elena_Danileiko 96–105 below left; harikarn 66–69 above left; Jaimie Duplass 86–89 above left; Joe Gough 85 above right; jxfzsy 18–29 below right; Lesyy 56–63 below right; loloalvarez 56–63 below left; loooby 96–105 above left; margouillatphotos 66–69 below left; Marilyn Barbone 86–89 below right; monkeybusinessimages 66–69 below right, 106–113 above right; oksix 36–39 below right; OlgaMiltsova 85 below right; Raul Taborda 18–29 above left; RonOrmanJr 56–63 above left; spflaum1 66–69 above right; tashka2000 18–29 above right; thawatpong 36–39 above left; Wiktory 46–49 above left; YelenaYemchuk 90–95 above left; Yulia Davidovich 80–83 below right.

Commissioning Editor Sarah Ford
Editor Pollyanna Poulter
Designer Jeremy Tilston
Picture Librarian Giulia Hetherington and Jennifer Veall
Production Controller Sarah-Jayne Johnson

Angela Dowden is a registered nutritionist, author and journalist and was voted Nutrition and Health LIVE writer/broadcaster of the year 2012.

Angela would like to thank Joeann Niblett for additional research.